DYLAN THOMAS

POET OF HIS PEOPLE

ANDREW SINCLAIR

MICHAEL JOSEPH

LONDON

This book was devised and produced by
Park and Roche Establishment, Schaan

Copyright © 1975 by Andrew Sinclair

First published in Great Britain in 1975 by
Michael Joseph Ltd, 52 Bedford Square, London WC1B 3EF

Designed by Crispin Fisher
Picture research by Juliet Brightmore

Printed in Italy by Amilcare Pizzi s.a., Milano

ISBN 0 7181 1438 8

Front jacket: *Portrait of Dylan Thomas by Augustus John.*

Back jacket: *View of Fishguard.*

Endpaper: *Dylan Thomas's manuscript for 'The Force That Through The Green Fuse', from the August 1933 notebook.*

Half-title: *Dylan Thomas in the dining-room of the Boat House, Laugharne, in 1953.*

Title-page: *Dylan Thomas in Millbrook, N.Y. in 1952.*

19 MAR 2003

22 OCT 2003

1 - DEC 2003

07 NOV 2007

02 JUL 2014

16 AUG 2017

CUMBRIA COUNTY LIBRARY

This book is due for return on or before the last date
above. It may be renewed by personal application,
post or telephone, if not in demand.

C.L.18

DYLAN THOMAS

Contents

Preface

I must first acknowledge with humility and gratitude the writings of Dylan Thomas himself, for no writer about Dylan can approach his own mocking appreciation of himself: his words have been lovingly preserved by his agents David Higham Associates and his literary executors, and carefully published by J. M. Dent & Sons. Caitlin Thomas's two books, *Leftover Life To Kill* (London, 1957) and *Not Quite Posthumous Letter To My Daughter* (London, 1963), show both a profound insight into Dylan's character and the greatness of her loss. Constantine Fitzgibbon's biography, *The Life of Dylan Thomas* (London, 1965), and his editing of *Selected Letters of Dylan Thomas* (London, 1966), put together most of the best material on the poet, and inform any reader with anecdote and intimation, reminiscence and insight. Bill Read's *The Days of Dylan Thomas* (London, 1965) puts a pleasant text between photographs of Dylan, mainly by Rollie McKenna, while John Malcolm Brinnin, *Dylan Thomas in America* (London, 1956) remains the unfortunate testimony of Dylan's fall to death. *Dylan Thomas, Letters to Vernon Watkins* (London, 1957) is a fine record of poetic craft and deep friendship.

Of the memoirs and appreciations of Dylan, far the best is John Ackerman's *Dylan Thomas : His Life and Work* (London, 1964), with its emphasis on Dylan's Welsh heritage. I am also indebted to Ralph Maud's scholarly work in *Poet in the Making : The Notebooks of Dylan Thomas* (London, 1968) and for his *Dylan Thomas in Print : a Bibliographical History* (London, 1970). Douglas Cleverdon's *The Growth of Under Milk Wood* (London, 1969) is also essential for a textual understanding of the play.

Beyond those books, information on Dylan is legion. I have been

Opposite: *Dylan Thomas in a wisteria creeper outside the home of Rollie McKenna in Millbrook, N.Y. in 1952.*

particularly and indirectly informed by Robert Graves in *The White Goddess* (London, 1961) about Welsh bards and minstrels, and more directly informed by the recent editions of Daniel Jones's *Dylan Thomas: The Poems* (London, 1971) and Walford Davies, *Dylan Thomas: Early Prose Writings* (London, 1971). While many modern critics love to tear apart the reputation of the greatest lyric poet of his time, those who illuminate his work are particularly Derek Stanford, *Dylan Thomas* (London, 1954); Henry Treece, *Dylan Thomas: Dog Among The Fairies* (London, 1956); Aneirin Talfan Davies, *Dylan: Druid of the Broken Body* (London, 1964); Clark Emery, *The World of Dylan Thomas* (London, 1971); and certain of the critics in Walford Davies ed: *Dylan Thomas: New Critical Essays* (London, 1972).

I am also indebted to hundreds of other writings on Dylan and to scores of friends for their accounts of him. By working for the Dylan Thomas Literary Executors on the dramatic version of *Adventures in the Skin Trade* and on the film version of *Under Milk Wood*, I was privileged to hear many stories and descriptions of Dylan. It would be invidious to single out any names from the many who have helped me. I can only thank them all most gratefully for their generous help to me over the past twenty years.

In the immediate preparation of this book, I can particularly thank my wife, Miranda Seymour, for her advice and help; Peter Bellew, for getting me to write the book; Juliet Brightmore and Christina Gascoigne for the pictorial insights; and Stanley Gebler Davies whose forthcoming biography of Dylan Thomas may be the most illuminating of them all.

Opposite: *Dylan at a rehearsal of* Under Milk Wood *in a New York apartment in 1953.*

Dylan Thomas

Before I Knocked

As yet ungotten, I did suffer;
The rack of dreams my lily bones
Did twist into a living cipher.
And flesh was snipped to cross the lines
Of gallow crosses on the liver
And brambles in the wringing brains . . .

And time cast forth my mortal creature
To drift or drown upon the seas
Acquainted with the salt adventure
Of tides that never touch the shores.
I who was rich was made the richer
By sipping at the vine of days.

from 'Before I Knocked' DYLAN THOMAS

Opposite: *The Royal National Eisteddfod of Wales in Bangor, 1902.*

Before I Knocked

To begin at the beginning.

The bards of ancient Wales were either master poets patronised at the Welsh courts or minstrels wandering from village to inn, telling their tales for bread and shelter. The court bards had to undergo a rigorous training in metre and metaphor and Christian allegory; a restricted official vocabulary, carefully vetted for heresy or indulgence, limited the abundance of the Welsh language; a ponderous classicism bound the Welsh tradition of the Middle Ages. Bards competed fiercely for the Chairs of Poetry at the various courts and for the patronage of the Welsh kings; but they were more courtiers than poets, more interested in a safe position than in the dangerous search after poetic truth. At one period, the court bards accepted a metrical code of writing, which restricted them in practice to writing eulogies of the princes and elegies for their deaths. The riches of the full Welsh language and its treasury of myths and romances were abandoned to the minstrels or travelling bards.

These were poets who wandered over the length and breadth of Wales, entertaining and prophesying, divining and telling stories, according to the principles of *The Red Book of Hergest*:

> Three things that enrich the poet:
> Myths, poetic power, a store of ancient verse.

The Norman invaders of the thirteenth century preferred the minstrels to the official bards of the Welsh courts. Thus the Welsh romances of Arthur and of chivalry spread through the Norman courts until they became the popular myths of all Europe. The new success of the minstrels allowed their more ancient and freer tradition to influence some official poetry in its turn. In the fifteenth century, just before the final fall of the independent Welsh princes, the poet Davydd ap Gwilym won official approval for the Kywydd, a form of poetry that united the

12

traditions of court bard and minstrel. The Welsh bardic tradition, however, collapsed during the English Civil Wars, and its revival in the National Eisteddfods today is rather laboured and influenced by Victorian reconstructions of the Druidic past. Even if the competition for the bardic Chair is as fierce as ever, the winning poems are as circumscribed and mannered as the official court poetry of medieval Wales.

This split bardic tradition was worsened by a split language. North Wales and mountain Wales remained Welsh-speaking and largely unconquered until Tudor times, while South Wales from Pembroke-shire to the English borders was held intermittently by Norman barons who first spoke in French and then in English. Thus the minstrels patronised by the invaders also learned to rhyme in a foreign language and, as the English language spread throughout Wales, particularly with the push of the industrial revolution through the valleys in the nineteenth century, so the common tongue of South Wales became English, the tongue of social advancement and working speech. The spread of nonconformity, too, with its chapels and English hymns, accustomed the people to sing in English as well as to swear at the English. So an economic and religious invasion from over the border led to the cultural dominance of England by the time of the First World War. The new breed of Welsh poets began to desert the tongue of their fathers for the words of the invaders.

One tradition survived in industrial Wales, the respect for the preacher and the poet. Even the coal mines were still situated by the villages, and the new towns and cities filled with people from farm families. Verses were appreciated and needed for burials. In his *Welsh Country Upbringing*, D. Parry Jones tells of visits to the local poet, a farm labourer and coal miner called Thomas, who composed churchyard memorial verses for all his part of Carmarthenshire. The elegies "though mournful in character and following the fashion and imitating the sentiments of hymns then popular, were full of gospel comfort . . . showing an extensive vocabulary and a mastery of diction, rhythm and rhyme." As for the rural preacher, he was the actor and judge of the whole community, causing the young Parry Jones to picture God "as a hard, merciless schoolmaster", able to see through his heart and mind, the cause of agony and fear to him all his life, an Almighty inescapable and ineffable. This awe of preachers and their methods of spreading the terror of God were caught by Dylan Thomas in his story 'The Peaches', where he tells of his cousin Gwilym preaching about hell-fire and the pit and the ever-watching Eye of God, to end on the words, "Thou canst see all the time. O God, mun, you're like a bloody cat."

Dylan M. Thomas was given the middle name of Marlais by his father. This was to commemorate the most famous member of this branch of the Thomas family, Dylan's great-uncle, Gwilym or William Thomas, who took the name of a bard from a stream in Cardiganshire, the Marles or Marlais. Gwilym was both preacher and bard, a radical and a Unitarian, the champion of Welsh tenants against their landlords, and a leading contributor to the Welsh periodicals of mid-Victorian times. For his support of the poor and the tenants he was evicted from his chapel, but he took his flock with him to a new chapel and achieved fame as a defender of the people. He was "the towering dead" remembered in Dylan Thomas's poem, and his influence lay strong on his nephew, Dylan's father, D. J. Thomas, who was not to escape the contradictions of Welsh society except through the person of his son.

D. J. Thomas's own father was a guard for the Great Western Railway, but he himself had the determination and many of the talents of the great Gwilym Marlais. He won a scholarship to the University of Wales in Aberystwyth, where he secured a First Class Honours degree in English. He wanted to be a poet, but he settled at the post of schoolmaster in English at Swansea Grammar School where he taught for nearly all of thirty-seven years until he retired in 1936. None of his private writings seems to have survived, only his anger at the waste of his talents through teaching, and his railing against God, for he was a life-long atheist in the manner of G. B. Shaw or H. G. Wells, holding even the weather against heaven and growling, "It's raining, blast Him!"

D. J. Thomas was the potential poet who lived in the no-man's land between the rural bard-and-preacher of the time of Gwilym Marlais and the urban rebellious poet of Dylan's time. His struggle to join the middle class and own a villa and bring up a family was too much for his talent at words, which were still-born. As Dylan's wife was to write, D. J. Thomas had to bear the strain of "the transition from farm house and railwaymen standards to schoolmaster in a semi-detached suburban matchbox . . . from lavish rough comforts to a pinched penny-pricing gentility."

His experience was that of much of Edwardian Wales. The urge of

Opposite: *Rain on the Taf estuary, Laugharne.*

Dylan's mother, Mrs Florence Thomas.

many of the Welsh for respectability at any price led to their reputation for hypocrisy. As though in fear of their dark desires, of their natural bawdiness, of their love of drink and chat and copulation, the majority of the Welsh after Wesley seem to have leapt first into a hell-fire puritanism and then into a suffocating respectability that was the condition of that blinkered, boxed, never-to-be-forgotten Swansea society, in which Dylan was born, from which he fled, against which he rebelled, out of which he could never escape. As he even complained at the height of his youthful revolt against the villa values of his home in Cwmdonkin Drive, all his poetry up to the age of eighteen seemed to have a "terrible lot of priggery in it – intellectual and emotional priggery." It read "like a chunk of adulterated Chesterton revised by Sir Edward Elgar." Even Dylan could not renege on the stern strictures of his youth.

Oddly enough, Dylan spoke no Welsh. There, again, he inherited the contradictions of the history of his country and his family. His father, who did speak Welsh, refused to teach his son the language, and even felt a certain contempt for those who did speak and write it. There was no question but that speaking Welsh in Swansea was a sign of not having quite arrived yet from the valleys or the mountains. It was somehow a little common. In Cwmdonkin Drive, Dylan's father and mother did not talk in the language of their parents or their youth. As a result, Dylan was steeped in the riches of the English language, although his rhythms and phrasings, his choice of metaphor and odd matchings of words, have that Celtic run and lilt which seems to percolate and press through the greatest writers of Ireland and Wales such as Joyce and Thomas, nightingales in an alien tongue that they better with the magic of their forgotten one.

If Dylan's father brought with him the urge to deny his Welsh working-class background, Dylan's mother always kept to the simpler standards of the farm. She was talkative, bright, generous, sociable, a worshipper at chapel and a lover of God, a wife who had little in common with her husband and much in common with humanity. She probably read no books except for the Bible and, in Constantine Fitzgibbon's opinion, she gave Dylan his "totally unformulated love of God", a half-way house between her warm, chapel-going heart and the conscious atheism of her husband. If Dylan in his late adolescence briefly despised her for being "stout, safe, confident, buried in her errands", his writings all show the love she brought into his life with her country ways and family, the uncles and aunts of 'A Child's Christmas in Wales', the "aged, peasant" Annie who lived at Fern Hill, Dosie who married a preacher, William the tenant farmer at the old home of Llangain.

Dylan Marlais Thomas was himself born on 27 October, 1914, in the house where he would live all his childhood and youth, 5 Cwmdonkin Drive, on the top of a hill by a park in the suburban district of Swansea called the Uplands. He had a sister, eight and half years older than him, called Nancy, who was too advanced to be much of a companion and who represented a new generation that was never to know very well the dream of rural Wales, which Dylan hymned and loved as it was losing ground. In his most rebellious book, *Adventures in the Skin Trade*, the anti-hero Sam Bennet rips up his sister's photograph and "down went the Girls' School and the long-legged, smiling colts with their black knickers and bows; the hockey-legged girls who laughed behind their hands." In real life, Dylan seems to have had a remote relationship

17

with his sister, because of the gap in age and sex and interests. She hardly appears in his writings or his life.

Dylan's name was his father's choice and it came from the *Mabinogion*, that Old Testament of Welsh myth. In the text, the son of a magician king makes a maiden, who claims to be a virgin, step over a magic wand. She drops a fine male child with yellow hair. Then the son of the magician says: "I shall name this child, and the name I shall give him is Dylan." Once named, the boy makes for the sea and becomes part of the sea, swimming as fast as the swiftest fish. "And for that reason he was called Dylan Eil Ton, Sea Son of the Wave." Curiously enough, Dylan's wife was to write that he had a definite connection with the fish family with his heavy hulk-shaped head and elongated, utterly useless hands which she was to call fins.

Dylan himself claimed that his name meant "the prince of darkness", but this mistake sounds like one of his exaggerations for effect. What is interesting in the choice of the son's names by the father is that both Dylan and Marlais were pre-Christian names, both dealt with magic and myth, both were bardic and both had to do with the mystery of water, the big seas and the rivers of dreams that were to haunt Dylan's imaginings. It is possible that by this choice of forenames, D. J. Thomas was electing Dylan Marlais Thomas to the fleshly chair of poetry where he himself would never sit.

This was the heritage of Dylan Thomas. His birthright was a divided country, a divided tradition, a divided language, a divided society, a divided house. As a Welshman, he was born to a land split between the stern nonconformist rural tradition of the naturalist north and the mountains, and the softer English growth of the southern towns and cities. As a bard, he inherited the formal respect for rhyme and discipline of the old court poets, and the opposed gifts of the minstrels, wandering and roistering where they could find ears to hear them. As a speaker of English, Dylan always had Welsh in his blood and heard the waves of Swansea's "two-tongued sea". As a social animal, Dylan was a hidden puritan, who expected women to be as neat as robins' eggs, and was even anxious about his wife's proper dressing when they went to the shops; but, equally, he was the mighty drinker and rioter, heir of the ancient feasts and the dark pubs of Swansea, the pig in the middle between the new middle-class and the old ways of farm and railway and mine. And, finally, he was caught at home between the fierce, disappointed education of his father and the warm, gabbing ignorance of his mother, who spoiled him, so that he never could discipline himself to the demands of his "craft or sullen art".

These coiled tensions, of course, made the contradictory poet in Dylan, who was indeed "dressed to die" before "the sensual strut begun". He was born into conflicts that he could never end except through his work of words, his endless search for a synthesis that was impossible, a unity in divergence, a sweet final resolution of the soul. As he was to write at eighteen, "To hell with everything except the inner necessity for expression and the medium of expression, everything except the great need of forever striving after this mystery and meaning I moan about. There is only one object: the removing of veils from your soul and scabs from your body." Dylan was to seek especially in his life that impossible freedom from his self, from the chains of his inheritance, which had willy-nilly helped to determine the poet, before he

> knocked and flesh let enter,
> With liquid hands tapped on the womb.

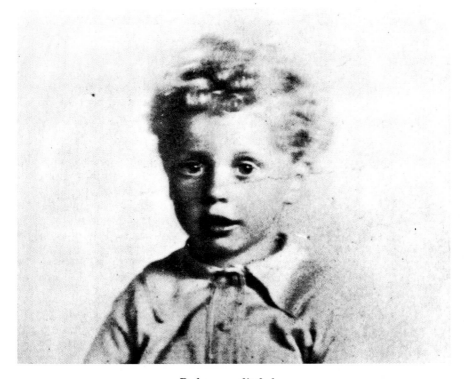

Dylan as a little boy.

Cwmdonkin Drive, Swansea.

Green as Beginning

This sea-town was my world; outside a strange Wales, coal-pitted, mountained, river run, full so far as I knew, of choirs and football teams and sheep and story-book tall black hats and red flannel petticoats, moved about its business which was none of mine . . . . And the park itself was a world within the world of the sea-town.

from 'Reminiscences of Childhood' DYLAN THOMAS

Green as Beginning

The world of a child is as big as his eyes. The first limits of small Dylan's "utterly confining outer world" were the front and back of 5 Cwmdonkin Drive, a new narrow semi-detached villa built in 1914, with the plaster still wet on its bricks while his mother's milk was wet on Dylan's lips. There was flowered paper on the walls, mock-ebony horses holding up the mantlepiece clock, willow-pattern china, tea-cosies and all the furniture of Welsh respectability. Two elements were unusual, D. J. Thomas's study lined with books, and the plaster reproductions of Greek statues. There were four rooms up and four down, with a narrow corridor serving them all. Dylan's home was part of the "ugly, lovely town" of Swansea on its seven little hills, "crawling, sprawling, slummed, unplanned, jerry-villa'd, and smug-suburbed by the side of a long and splendid-curving shore."

Beyond the house, however, lay the steep slip down to sea, and the upper windows showed a slope of slate roofs that plunged down to the bay and the harbour, with the Mumbles Head Lighthouse a sentinel to the west. The house itself was perched awry on the hill, threatening to toboggan down on any wild wet day, but facing a reservoir topped with grass and a playing field, beyond which lay the little tree-lined Cwmdonkin Park, "full of terrors and treasures . . . as many secret places, caverns and forests, prairies and deserts, as a country somewhere at the end of the sea."

This park was to become the Africa and the Arctic of the small boy Dylan and his rascal friends. His usual approach to its jungles was to force his way directly under the wire that shut the park off from the reservoir, then to crawl through the back into the giant firs, so oddly mingling with palmettos and yuccas and monkey-puzzle trees. Ignored were the respectable parts of the park, the rose garden and the tennis

Opposite: *Swansea and the Mumbles from Cwmdonkin Park.*

courts and the bowling green. But by the fountain where boy Dylan sailed his model boats was the rockery and "the loud zoo of the willow groves". There Dylan located the Hunchback of his poem, who

Made all day until bell time
A woman figure without fault
Straight as a young elm
Straight and tall from his crooked bones
That she might stand in the night
After the locks and chains

All night in the unmade park
After the railings and shrubberies
The birds the grass the trees the lake
And the wild boys innocent as strawberries
Had followed the hunchback
To his kennel in the dark.

It was into that park that boy Dylan followed the Thomases' living proof that they had arrived – Patricia, the servant who lived in the semi-detached house. His story, 'Patricia, Edith and Arnold', describes Patricia as a "tall, thick girl with awkward hands", with fingers like toes and shoulders wide as a man's, given to spoiling him. And he needed spoiling at times, for he was often ill as a child. He suffered from weak lungs and had to keep to his bed for weeks on end, because of haemorrhages. Here he developed a voracious taste for reading, a talent for truancy and avoiding examinations, and a firm conviction that he would die young of consumption. In fact, his scarred lungs healed, and it was asthma and excessive smoking after the age of fifteen that led to his thundering cough and frequent wheezing for breath, even though he liked to claim that he had "already had twice as much of it as Keats had".

These bouts in bed did, however, interrupt his early schooldays at Mrs Hole's School in Mirador Crescent, three blocks down the hill towards the harbour. It was a private school, socially superior and educationally inferior to the State primary school; but middle-class children were sent there. Dylan's friend Mervyn Levy was at Mirador Crescent at the same age as Dylan and declared that they learned nothing there at all. Yet Dylan wrote of his memories there with affection. It was "firm and kind and smelling of galoshes". And he did learn more than boasting and smoking the butt-ends of cigarettes with the other boys. As the First Voice declares in *Return Journey*: "In Mirador School he learned to read and count. Who made the worst raffia doilies? Who put water in Joyce's galoshes, every morning prompt as prompt? In the afternoons, when the children were good, they read aloud from Struwelpeter. And when they were bad, they sat alone in the empty classroom, hearing, from above them, the distant, terrible, sad music of the late piano lesson."

Between the dame-school and the park and the house, in which only pencils and paper could confine Dylan when it was wet, the small boy lived, unless he was invited away to the farm at Fern Hill or to Aunt Dosie's manse at Newton, where there was too much Sunday School to compensate for the green glories of occasional outings to the Gower Peninsula. At Llangain, however, where the remote farm stood under Fern Hill, Dylan was really "young and easy under the apple boughs about the lilting house and happy as the grass was green." The farm in its coat of yellow wash sprawled round three sides of a court, with the farmyard and outbuildings to one side. Like Cwmdonkin Drive, the farm stood on a slope and the ground dropped away sharply to a lower stream past an old flower-garden. Like Cwmdonkin Park, the farmhouse was surrounded by tall old trees, the survivors of that Milk Wood which once used to cover nearly all of ancient Wales. Although the house smelt of rotten wood and damp and animals, the kitchen was lamp-lit and warm, and Aunt Annie loved Dylan, and he played the summer days away in byre and field, on cart and hill.

> And as I was green and carefree, famous among the barns
> About the happy yard and singing as the farm was home,
>> In the sun that is young once only,
>>> Time let me play and be
>>> Golden in the mercy of his means . . .

Yet the poem of 'Fern Hill' is the older Dylan's nostalgia for his roustabout country holidays, while his opening story in *Portrait of the Artist as a Young Dog*, 'The Peaches', reveals more of the fears and taints of childhood, that Welsh sense of sin and wickedness that was a hidden anchor always in Dylan's free soul. In this, young Dylan listens to his cousin Idris (whom the story calls Gwilym like Gwilym Marlais, the bard-preacher), as he practises his preaching from a farm-cart and then descends to take confessions from his congregation of two small boys, pointing his finger and asking for the worst crime they had done. The boy Dylan catalogues his crimes to himself, letting another boy be

25

Mrs Florence Thomas at Fern Hill.

whipped for taking his homework, stealing from his mother's handbag, filching library books and throwing them away in the park, drinking his own water to see what it tasted like, beating a dog with a stick to make it lick his hand, looking with a friend through the keyhole to see his maid having a bath, saying that blood on his handkerchief came out of his ears to frighten his mother, pulling his trousers down to show Jack Williams, breaking into a house to pour ink over the bedclothes – all the crimes of a naughty small boy, that weigh him down for fear of being found out, crimes that he will never confess, except to another boy; the huge burden of trivial sin so heavy on the young, if hell-fire is threatened as well; the awful sense of unnecessary guilt that afflicts the Welsh conscience, young and old.

There was another dark side to the farmhouse at Fern Hill – the story of the Hangman. In legend, a Hangman had lived there with a beautiful daughter, who tried to run away with her lover while he

went off to do his killing jobs in Carmarthen jail. The Hangman barred
up the lower rooms and made a prisoner of the girl, but at the last
she slipped away. So he hanged himself in the kitchen up the hall.
Dylan often told this boy-scaring tale with relish later in his life, and
it was one of the influences that lay behind his perennial gothic fantasies,
to be revealed in one letter of 1932 when he looked out into the decent
Swansea street outside his window and saw "ghouls, vampires, women-
rippers, deflowerers of weeny infants, warted soaks, pimps and financiers
pass by." Particularly in the stories in *The Map of Love* and in those
collected in his *Early Prose Writings* does this excessive, morbid, dark
streak appear, a prying after incest, after babies bloodied and burning,
after a school of witches learning "the intricate devil", where a black
scissorman "bent over Gladwys, he healed her wound, she stood his
ointment and his fire, she burned at the true altar, and the black
sacrifice was done." Only in the pubs could Dylan later laugh away his
fears of witchcraft, claiming to have seen Aleister Crowley sitting in
his own bath water.

So much for the visions of glory and damnation from Fern Hill and
the manse at Newton. The boy Dylan chiefly lived in the town of
Swansea, where the streets and the beach were the escape of the
schoolboy, just as the park had been the refuge and battleyard of the
small boy. It was a "splendidly ugly sea town" to the children, roaming
it in search of adventures. As Dylan later declared:

> with my friends, I used to dawdle on half-holidays along the
> bent and Devon-facing seashore, hoping for corpses or gold
> watches or the skull of a sheep or a message in a bottle to be
> washed up in the wrack; or where we used to wander, whistling
> and being rude to strangers, through the packed streets,
> stale as station sandwiches, around the impressive gas-works
> and the slaughter-house, past the blackened monuments of
> civic pride and the museum, which should have been in a
> museum; where we scratched at a kind of cricket on the bald
> and cindery surface of the recreation-ground, or winked at
> unapproachably old girls of fifteen or sixteen on the promenade
> opposite; where we took a tram that shook like an iron jelly
> down from our neat homes to the gaunt pier, there to clamber
> *under* the pier, hanging perilously on its skeleton-legs; or to
> run along to the end where patient men with the seaward
> eyes of the dockside unemployed, capped and muffered,

dangling from their mouths pipes that had long gone out, angled over the edge for unpleasant tasting fish. Never *was* there such a town as ours, I thought.

As for the Grammar School, though, it was the same as all other schools to Dylan, except that his father taught English there. From the age of four years old, Dylan had been read Shakespeare by his father in his study, long before the words had meaning, but were only sound after sound, signifying thunders and wondrous nothings. Now in the Grammar School, under a wise and progressive headmaster who did not force the pupils to learn against their grain, but only what seemed of use to them, Dylan studied English and nothing much else. He early found out that he hated academic disciplines, although he later regretted his lack of languages and professional training, and he lived in fear of his ignorance being found out. But while at school, except for some extraordinary victories in long-distance running races, which gave him pride all his life, he was bad at his work and not particularly distinguished among his fellows, being small and slight and making up for his size by his boasting and daring. In *Return Journey*, he put a description of himself into the mouth of a schoolmaster:

> Oh yes, I remember him well, the boy you are
>   searching for:
> he looked like most boys, no better, brighter, or more
>   respectful;
> he cribbed, mitched, spilt ink, rattled his desk and
> garbled his lessons with the worst of them;
> he could smudge, hedge, smirk, wriggle, wince,
> whimper, blarney, badger, blush, deceive, be
> devious, stammer, improvise, assume
> offended dignity or righteous indignation as though
>   to the manner born . . .
> . . . he scuffled at prayers,
> he interpolated, smugly, the time-honoured wrong
> irreverent words into the morning hymns,
> he helped to damage the headmaster's rhubarb,
> was thirty-third in trigonometry,
> and, as might be expected, edited the School Magazine.

Opposite: "*. . . the bent and Devon-facing seashore . . .*"

There was nothing much else that Dylan did for Swansea Grammar School, or that the school did for him. More important to Dylan than formal work was the friendship he found with Daniel Jones, who was to become his accomplice, inspirer and best friend. The relationship began with the fight at the age of fourteen described in *Portrait of the Artist as a Young Dog*. A strange boy pushes Dylan down a bank, they wrestle and rabbit-punch, they scratch and bite, they give each other a nose-bleed and a black eye, then they turn to throw gravel at a man in his garden, egging them on, before walking away together. Dylan leaves his own room with his exercise-book full of poems and its pictures of Shakespeare, Walter de la Mare, Robert Browning, Stacy Aumonier, Rupert Brooke, John Greenleaf Whittier, Watts's 'Hope', and a Sunday School certificate, which he is too ashamed to take down. He marches over to Daniel Jones's room, impressed by his new friend's claims to be a composer and a poet, the writer of seven historical novels before the age of twelve, and a piano-player and a violinist too. The Joneses' house, called Warmley, in Eversley Road was to become Dylan's second home, where he and Daniel would play fierce cricket and run a mock radio station between upstairs and downstairs, specialising in such talks as "Locomotive Bowen, the one-eyed cowhand, will give a talk on the Rocking Horse and Varnishing Industry."

So, befriended and secure in his home comforts, Dylan lived out his youth, in his outer world of Swansea, swaggering and blustering and pretending all the time to be the man he was not yet. He liked putting on many faces to please, the pouting angel when in trouble, the loquacious poet when seeking to impress, the doomed consumptive when asking for sympathy, the bold drinker and smoker among his companions, and the would-be lover among the girls. Later he would mock his pretensions of that time in *Return Journey*, putting in the mouths of the answering girls that he sounded as if he had "swallowed a dictionary" with his "cut-glass accent and father's trilby".

No question but schoolboy Dylan felt that lonely certainty of talent, that bravado on the face of inexperience, that unnecessary need to impose his manhood on all and sundry, which is the mark of the bright adolescent in his elementary town and suburban situation. Dylan's saving grace beneath his bluster and arrogance was his sense of humour. He never could take himself as seriously as he wished he could. This vein of self-mockery is best shown in the little parody of his life, written to Pamela Hansford Johnson in 1933 from Cwmdonkin Drive. It is headed 'A Touching Autobiography In One Paragraph'.

I first saw the light of day in a Glamorgan villa, and, amid the terrors of the Welsh accent and the smoke of the tinplate stacks, grew up to be a sweet baby, a precocious child, a rebellious boy, and a morbid youth. My father was a school-master: a broader-minded man I have never known. My mother came from the agricultural depths of Carmarthen-shire: a pettier woman I have never known. My only sister passed through the stages of long-legged schoolgirlishness, shortfrocked flappery and social snobbery into a comfortable married life. I was first introduced to Tobacco (the Boy Scout's Enemy) when a small boy in a preparatory school, to alcohol (the Demon King) when a senior member of a second-ary school. Poetry (the Spinster's Friend) first unveiled herself to me when I was six or seven years old; she still remains, though sometimes her face is cracked across like an old saucer . . .

So wrote Dylan on himself from the vantage point of eighteen years old in this mock-Welsh tract to his new London love. What he said was not quite true, for he embroidered on events for the love of them. A later sentence in this excuse for an autobiography reads, "A misanthropic doctor, who apparently did not like the way I did my eyebrows, has given me four years to live." Jeering at his fears, with his tongue in his reader's cheek, self-parodying as well as self-important, Dylan left school at sixteen and a half to earn his bread by his words, or waste of them.

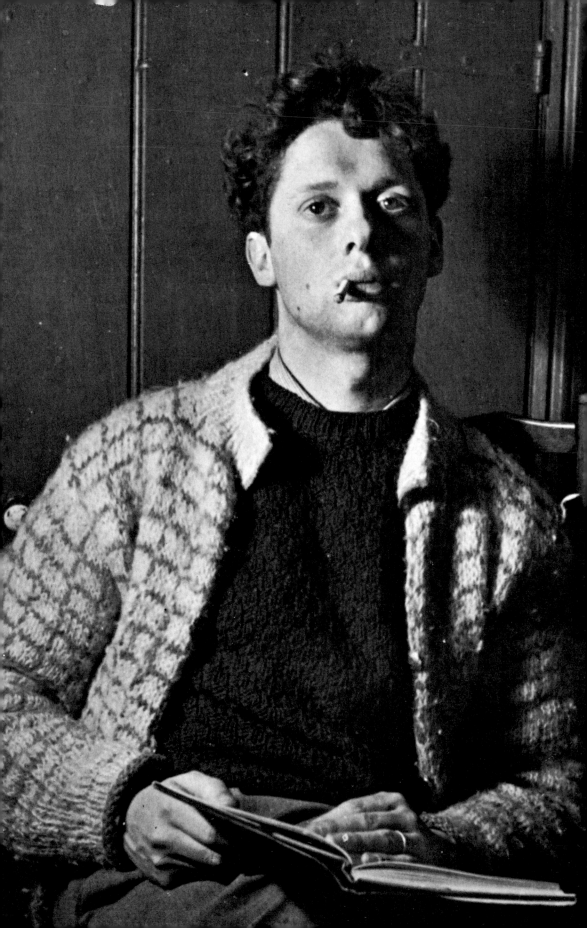

A Bombastic Adolescent Provincial Bohemian

Few understand the works of Cummings,
And few James Joyce's mental slummings,
And few young Auden's coded chatter;
But then it is the few that matter.
Never be lucid, never state,
If you would be regarded great,
The simplest thought or sentiment,
(For thought, we know, is decadent) . . .

from 'A Letter to my Aunt Discussing the Correct Approach to
Modern Poetry' DYLAN THOMAS

Opposite: *'Dylan wore "a conscious Woodbine"'*.

A Bombastic Adolescent
Provincial Bohemian

In Swansea in the depression in 1931, Dylan was lucky to get a job. The city was full of youths hanging around on the dole, such as the two brothers in 'Just Like Little Dogs', who stand silent for hours under the railway arch, "statues smoking, tough-capped and collarless watchers and witnesses . . . with nowhere to go, nothing to do." Dylan was taken on as a copy boy, then as a junior reporter, by the *South Wales Daily Post*. For fifteen months, he read proofs before taking to the streets to report local events, such as weddings and fires and funerals. As a reporter, he was both evasive and inaccurate, finding out that all events were much the same, if he left out the list of names of those attending, which he did. The time saved from the working day was spent in the Y.M.C.A. billiards hall or in the Kardomah café, where he met his friends and argued the toss, chatting the 'thirties to death. As he wrote in *Return Journey*, he and the young lounge lizards talked about: "Communism, symbolism, Bradman, Braque, the Watch Committee, free love, free beer, murder, Michelangelo, ping-pong, ambition, Sibelius, and girls. . . . How Dan Jones was going to compose the most prodigious symphony, Fred Janes paint the most miraculously meticulous picture, Charlie Fisher catch the poshest trout, Vernon Watkins and Young Thomas write the most boiling poems, how they would ring the bells of London and paint it like a tart . . ."

When he was on the job, Dylan used to try and imitate the movie newshound or senior reporter, Fred Farr, a pub-crawler who knew his way round the prim face and the grim underbelly of Swansea. In imitation of his teacher of high and low life, Dylan wore "a conscious Woodbine" on his lower lip, a check overcoat, a porkpie hat and a reporter's slouch, as he gathered more beer in his gut than news in his head. His beat was the Swansea mainly of the pubs, either The Three Lamps, "that snug, smug, select Edwardian holy of best-bitter holies", or the dark dock bars described in 'Old Garbo', a fug of chat and warm

34

drunkenness that was to hold Dylan all of his life with "the taste of beer, its live, white lather, its brass-bright depths, the sudden world through the wet brown walls of the glass, the tilted rush to the lips and the slow swallowing down to the lapping belly."

During this time, Dylan was writing poetry, but it was the poetry of his first two *Notebooks*, still imitative and unworked. By the Christmas of 1932, the editor of the newspaper and Dylan agreed to part, with Dylan contributing occasional articles as a free-lance on such subjects as the Poets of Swansea. His reason for giving up his job had been confessed to Trevor Hughes in the February of that year. "I am at the most transitional period now. Whatever talents I possess may suddenly diminish or may suddenly increase. I can, with great ease, become an ordinary fool. I may be one now. But it doesn't do to upset one's own vanity." Certainly the gap in the *Notebooks* and the weaker Surrealist and drunken poems date from this period, when Dylan was playing news-hawk.

Once Dylan had decided to be a poet, impure and unsimple, and to work at little else, he drafted and nearly completed most of the best poems in his first volume, *18 Poems*, and nearly half of those in *Twenty-five Poems*, published in 1936, and *The Map of Love*, published in 1939. He drew his local encouragement from the writers' circle which met twice a week at the house of Bert Trick, a local Socialist organiser and editor, who actually lived off the proceeds of a small grocer's down the hill from Cwmdonkin Drive and "threatened the annihilation of the ruling classes over sandwiches and jelly and blancmange." Trick and his wife urged Dylan to read his poems and have them published, if he could. They also developed his talent for the theatrical delivery of his work. Their summer bungalow on the Gower Peninsula was a favourite refuge of Dylan's, where he could walk for miles by the sea and forget the suburban constraints of his home.

This small provincial circle, so important for Dylan in his isolation, was movingly mocked by him in his story, 'Where Tawe Flows'. There the budding writers meet like conspirators in the small villa and wait for the wife to go to bed before embarking on their long collaborative novel. Dylan always liked writing prose in company, forced by others to the convivial pen; at various times, he wrote alternate lines or pages of works with Daniel Jones, Vernon Watkins and John Davenport. The title of his story about the writers' circle is the title of their novel in common, and the plotters are called to order as if at a Labour Party meeting, while the Minutes are read by Mr Thomas, being the substance of the book.

"Any questions, gentlemen?" he then asks, and an evening of irrelevant story-telling develops between the comrades.

The comfortable gentility of Swansea life, even among its rebels and would-be artists, was initially a cradle for Dylan's talent although later, in the first days of his Soho rebellion, it would seem as suffocating as the villa home which Sam Bennet destroys in *Adventures in the Skin Trade* before running away to the big smoke of London. However anarchic Dylan was to be, he could never overcome his gratitude and guilt for that safe, prissy, known Swansea world of dreams in doilies, rebellions in parlours, radicalism in beer-mugs. Like Sam Bennet burning his mother's sunshade to prove his escape from her, Dylan would always feel shame when he denied his puritan upbringing and his appreciation of the niceties of women, tasting his tears like Sam and saying, "It's salt. It's very salt. Just like in my poems."

With Bert Trick's encouragement, Dylan began to have his poems published. It was rare, indeed, that any magazine refused a Thomas work. His first major poem to be printed was 'That Sanity Be Kept', the second was 'The Force That Through The Green Fuse Drives The Flower' with its terrible Blakeian lines:

> And I am dumb to tell the crooked rose
> My youth is bent by the same wintry fever.

In all, Victor Neuberg, who ran a poetry half-column in the London *Sunday Referee*, was to print seven of Dylan's poems between 1933 and 1935, along with poems by David Gascoyne and Pamela Hansford Johnson.

It was this London connection and correspondence with Miss Johnson, then known as a young poetress, which took Dylan to the capital in 1933 on a reconnaissance and in 1934 on a longer stay. The letters between the two young writers show Dylan at the age of nineteen to be bombastic for fear of seeming provincial, world-weary in case he was thought naïve, tough to disguise tenderness, and sexually aware to hide a probable virginity. Dylan's biographer, Constantine Fitzgibbon, has testified to the poet's masturbation throughout his life, and his early poems certainly reveal that tendency, particularly such lines in the *Notebooks* as:

> Jack my father let the knaves steal off
> Their little swag, the gems of life and death . . .

or the more explicit:

Pamela Hansford Johnson as a young writer.

Now that drugged youth is waking from its stupor,
The nervous hand rehearsing on the thigh
Acts with a woman . . .

Dylan's intense preoccupation with sexuality was a form of repression until his twenties, as he bitterly wrote to Miss Johnson in 1933, before he had met her. "My experience of waking with a woman at my side has been necessarily limited. The medieval laws of this corrupted hemisphere have dictated a more or less compulsory virginity during the period of life when virginity should be regarded as a crime against the dictates of the body." If this forced repression had not been true, Dylan would not have made such a vainglorious confession to Miss Johnson of his first known sexual encounter, a week-end in the Gower Peninsula with a friend and a girl called Jane with a loose red mouth. In this letter towards the end of his close relationship with Miss Johnson, Dylan showed the need to boast more than to ask forgiveness, to wallow in the splendour of his sin rather than to declare a deep love for his fellow-poet in London.

37

His drinking, too, was the young provincial poet's other pride. He loved to write of his feats with alcohol, as if somehow boozing was a proof of manhood, a denial of the chapel. An old saying was that the shortest way out of Birmingham was a bottle of gin. To the young Dylan, the best way out of Swansea seemed a bellyful of beer. He liked it when he could "sedulously pluck the flower of alcohol". To Pamela Hansford Johnson, he boasted both of delirium tremens and of being doomed to die from consumption within four years. Dylan's adolescent sense of drama crept into his letters from the amateur theatricals in which he loved to perform.

Those poets who are also actors are often popular in their lifetimes, because they can interpret their own works, bravura and pauses and all, to audiences who love rhetoric more than reading. Dylan on the platform was certainly his own best ambassador, although off it he could be his own worst diplomat. In this love of show, he was a people's poet, a true medieval minstrel. As his friend Richard Burton declared, all Welsh people are naturally actors, and only the worst ever become professional. Dylan's only interest at school other than English had been acting, where he had delivered a "fresh and clean" version of the aged Oliver Cromwell. Later, he had given rumbustious characterisations for the Mumbles Stage Society, playing in productions of Coward and Farquahar and Congreve. His friend Bert Trick witnessed how early Dylan's rich and sonorous style of reading poetry was developed, how its spells held its hearers.

It was to be Dylan's pride to act so well that, whatever the poem, his delivery of it would awe the audience. Richard Burton again has told of an evening spent with Dylan and Louis MacNeice, in which both he himself and MacNeice recited their favourite and most profound piece of poetry at Dylan's request. When asked for his own, Dylan slowly said, "This is the best poem in the English language," and then repeated gravely and with feeling these lines:

> I am
> Thou art
> He, she, it is
> We are
> You are
> They are.

According to Burton, the delivery of the lines was such that the words did seem to be the ultimate in all poetry.

Such was the adolescence of Dylan Thomas, before he began to leave Swansea increasingly for London and discard the image of himself as the tough provincial, to become the fallen angel of Fitzrovia that is captured in Augustus John's famous portrait of him. Luckily, Dylan has left an equally famous portrait of himself at the close of his Swansea youth, the mocking outer cover to the inner poet. "He'd be about seventeen or eighteen and above medium height. Above medium height for Wales, I mean, he's five foot six and a half. Thick blubber lips; snub nose; curly mousebrown hair; one front tooth broken after playing a game called Cats and Dogs, in the Mermaid, Mumbles; speaks rather fancy; truculent; plausible; a bit of a shower-off; plus-fours and no breakfast, you know; used to have poems printed in the *Herald of Wales*; there was one about an open-air performance of *Electra* in Mrs Bertie Perkins's garden in Sketty; lived up the Uplands; a bombastic adolescent provincial Bohemian with a thick-knotted artist's tie made out of his sister's scarf, she never knew where it had gone, and a cricket-shirt dyed bottle-green; a gabbing, ambitious, mock-tough, pretentious young man; and mole-y, too."

Dylan at Sea View, Laugharne.

Cwmdonkin Park, Swansea.

No Loving Shepherd

The plum my mother picked matured slowly,
The boy she dropped from darkness at her side
Into the sided lap of light grew strong,
Was muscled, matted, wise to the crying thigh
And to the voice that, like a voice of hunger,
Itched in the noise of wind and sun.

from 'Love's First Fever' DYLAN THOMAS

No Loving Shepherd

Dylan was born to be a poet. He never doubted that. Words were always his delight and his play. The things that first made him "love language and want to work *in* it and *for* it were nursery rhymes and folk tales, the Scottish Ballads, a few lines of hymns, the most famous Bible stories and the rhythms of the Bible, Blake's *Songs of Innocence*, and the quite incomprehensible magical majesty and nonsense of Shakespeare heard, read and near-murdered" in the first form of his school.

Before Dylan could understand the meaning of words, he loved them for their sound. They occupied his mind, as his boyhood friend Daniel Jones said, to the exclusion even of the things connected with them. Dylan pursued this work of words at school without caring for anything else. He failed every examination in Senior Certificate except English, which his father taught and which he loved. He was truant at all learning that did not have to do with the art of poetry, either writing it or speaking it.

The contrast between Dylan's editorship of the *Swansea Grammar School Magazine*, in which he wrote bright light verse, and his *First Notebook* of poetry, which he began at the age of fifteen and a half, reflects the split in his nature between the public D. M. Thomas, schoolmaster's son with a social face and the parlour standards of suburban Swansea, and the secret youth of Dylan, bawdy and bardic in his bedroom alone. His first published poem is called 'The Song of the Mischievous Dog' and reads like Lewis Carroll minor. It begins:

> There are many who say that a dog has its day,
> And a cat has a number of lives;
> There are others who think that a lobster is pink,
> And that bees never work in their hives . . .

The only hint of Dylan's more hidden desires comes in the final lines:

42

> . . . And if I indulge in a bite at a bulge
> Let's hope you won't think me too vicious.

But this facile rhyming for public view was privately contradicted in the groping of the free-style poems of the *First* and *Second Notebooks*. These poems are a curious mixture of imitations from the Elizabethans and Beddoes, Tennyson and Walter de la Mare, Sacheverell Sitwell and the early W. B. Yeats, allied with the wants and despairs and violent obscurities that were to become a feature of the mature poet. While the urge to shock is everywhere in lines such as "your thighs burning with pressure" or "this pus runs deep . . . On every hand the evil's positive," even the blasphemy has a lyrical quality that was to set the later poet in that special green heaven and hell of his, urgent on the themes of love and death and spring and God. He was just sixteen when he wrote the first draft of 'How Shall My Animal'. Except for the first line, little of Dylan's work or self as a terrible youth, the Rimbaud of Cwmdonkin Drive, survives into the final poem, except for his adolescent sexual urge seeking to link religion and women in a fusion of holy lust. This is the youth's version:

> . . . My senses see.
> Speak then, o body, shout aloud,
> And break my only mind from chains
> To go where ploughing's ended.
> The dancing women all lie down;
> Their turning wheels are still as death;
> No hope can make them glad,
> Lifting their cheery bodies as before
> In many shapes and signs,
> A cross of legs
> Poor Christ was never nailed upon,
> A sea of breasts,
> A thousand sailing thighs . . .

This is the final version of the adolescent thoughts of sea and crucifixion and lust, published eight years later when Dylan was in his flower:

> . . . I with a living skein,
> Tongue and ear in the thread, angle the temple-bound
> Curl-locked and animal cavepools of spells and bone,
> Trace out a tentacle,
> Nailed with an open eye, in the bowl of wounds and weed

To clasp my fury on ground
And clap its great blood down;
Never shall beast be born to atlas the few seas
Or poise the day on a horn.

The early poems of the *First Notebook*, indeed, stand on their own. They are merely markers of the method that the poet was to use. Although Dylan wasted words riotously in his speech, he wrought them with labyrinthine care in the drafts of his finished and published and self-chosen *Collected Poems* of 1952, which were all he wished to preserve up until that time, less than two years before his early death. His way of working was both disorganised and elaborate. As he wrote in 1935 to a friend, Charles Fisher: "My method is this: I write a poem on innumerable sheets of scrap paper, write it on both sides of the paper, often upside down and criss cross ways unpunctuated, surrounded by drawings of lamp posts and boiled eggs, in a very dirty mess, bit by bit I copy out the slowly developing poem into an exercise book; and, when it is completed, I type it out. The scrap sheets I burn . . ."

Later in his life, Dylan would keep the fragments, but he would copy out a poem laboriously in longhand every time that he changed it. He was to show John Malcolm Brinnin two hundred separate and distinct versions of 'Fern Hill'. This was his way of keeping the poem together, so that it grew like an organism. As he was to tell Brinnin, he carried a phrase in his head for many years, and if it was resonant or pregnant, it would suggest another phrase. So the poem would accumulate through draft after draft, year after year, until at last he found it sufficient.

The *Second, Third* and *Fourth Notebooks*, which largely cover Dylan's drafts for poems between 1930 and 1934, were used by him as sources for his poems as late as 1941. They show a young poet's mind developing from a vocabulary of gloom and imitative Surrealism – probably the product of his first job on the *South Wales Daily Post*. His attempts at protest poetry in the manner of W. H. Auden are failures, with obvious references such as "the living dead left over from the war" or "the Western man with one lung gone". But the surging lines of the future poems are already there, including an early draft of 'And death shall have no dominion'. His search continues for the antithesis of Welsh puritanism, with its insistence on righteousness and a severe God, who cannot be questioned.

Opposite: *Portrait of Dylan Thomas by Alfred Janes.*

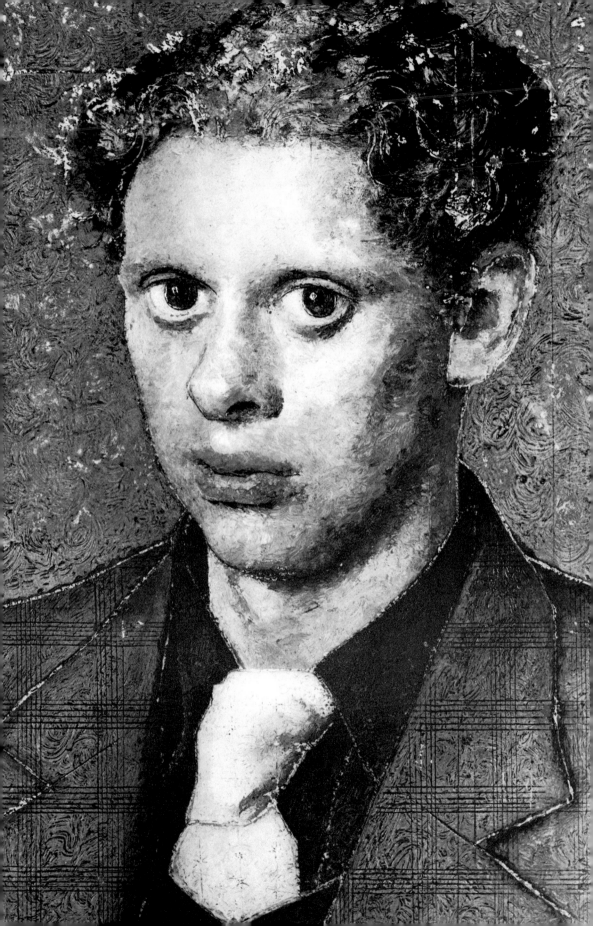

Where, what's my God among this crazy rattling
Of knives on forks, he cried, of nerve on nerve,
Man's ribs on woman's, straight line on a curve,
And hand to buttock, man to engine, battling,
Bruising, where's God's my Shepherd, God is Love?
No loving shepherd in this upside life.

Veering between belief and despair, most of the later poems of the
Notebooks show Dylan's early search for a mystical fusion of the
contradictions that were to torment him all his life. He could not
wholly reject the censorious society that loved him, while longing
fiercely for the appalling freedom of the poet. He could not spurn God,
although he boasted in 1933 that God had been deposed years ago and
the Devil reigned. He could only try to resolve the conflicts between the
outer obvious world, which had to be lived in and enjoyed and endured,
and between his inner vision of some impossible unity in creation. The
knowledge of the artist was "of the actual world's deplorable sordidness,
and of the invisible world's splendour." Even Dylan's own poems did
not seem satisfactory to him because they dealt too much with the
necessary outer world. "Perhaps the greatest works of art are those that
reconcile, perfectly, inner and outer."

The *Fourth* and final *Notebook* marks the certainty of Dylan with his
life-long preoccupation, an emphasis on the body as the arbiter of all
things, a view criticised by his new friend Pamela Hansford Johnson.
To Dylan, the body was both meaty and metaphysical as it had been for
John Donne and William Blake. "Every idea, intuitive or intellectual,
can be imaged and translated in terms of the body, its flesh, skin, blood,
sinews, veins, glands, organs, cells, or senses." Even the extra-ter-
restrial could be described in terms of the body; in fact it must be so
described by Dylan, because he could not rise to the stars. He had "to
bring down the stars" to his own level. He was the opposite of Plato, who
wrote of his lost love:

My Star, you are raised to the stars in the skies.
O, to see you as the heaven does with many eyes.

Dylan preferred his "unpretty" poems with an "imagery almost totally
anatomical . . . the perhaps wearisome succession of blood and bones,
the never ending similes of the streams in the veins and the lights in the
eyes." To him, in the final *Notebook*, there was a "firmament of flesh and
bone". Jesus Christ, indeed, became the key to this mystery of God in

man, even to the agnostic and doubting Thomas, whose poems of the period were awash with the blood and the body and the pain of the crucifixion. Yet, finally, Dylan was always the heretic, the Averroist, believing that part of the godhead was somehow in every body, that each being was somehow his own suffering Jesus. Spirituality had to be totally comprehended in the experience of living. As he declared at the end of the last *Notebook*, "Man be my metaphor."

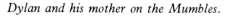

Dylan and his mother on the Mumbles.

47

Miss Johnson

Hints for Recognition

    *The gradual shrinking you complain of is chiefly
mental, for the more despondent I become the littler and
weaker I feel.*

    Height—five foot six (about).
    Weight—eight stone ten (about).
    Hair   —some sort of rat-coloured brown.
    *Eyes   —big, brown and green (this sounds as though one
              were brown & the other green; the colours
              are mixed).*
    *Distinguishing Marks—Three moles on right cheek,
                  scar on arm and ankle, though
                  as I generally wear socks you
                  won't see the little mark there.*
    Sex   —male, I think.
    *Voice   —I suppose it would be called baritone, though
              sometimes it sweeps towards tenor and
              sometimes droops towards bass. Except in
              moments of hilarity, I believe I speak without
              an accent.*
    Size of Feet—five (this is not number).
    Cigarettes   —Players, forty a day stuck in centre of mouth.
    Food   —Hay.

    from a letter to Pamela Hansford Johnson by Dylan Thomas,
                      written in late 1933

Opposite: *Dylan Thomas sent this photograph of himself to Pamela Hansford
Johnson in 1933.*

Miss Johnson

Miss Pamela Hansford Johnson was a young poet, who was sometimes published by the eccentric Victor Neuberg in the Poets' Corner of the *Sunday Referee*. In the summer of 1933, she read a poem by the unknown Dylan Thomas, which began:

> That sanity be kept I sit at open windows,
> Regard the sky, make unobtrusive comment on the moon,
> Sit at open windows in my shirt,
> And let the traffic pass, the signals shine,
> The engines run, the brass bands keep in tune,
> For sanity must be preserved.

It was not a good poem, echoing Auden and Eliot, but it was good enough to make Miss Johnson write to Swansea in search of Dylan. His reply is preserved. He dispraises the poems which she encloses, but he returns to her more of his own poems. He is glad that she is not an aged virgin, but the same immodest age as himself – in fact, Dylan lied, for he was two years younger. His reply was enough to unclench a correspondence between the young writers that is as remarkable as it is one-sided, for Dylan kept none of her letters, while she kept all of his.

Both young poets were frustrated, she by working in an office, he by feeling ignored in Wales. At home, Dylan's friends were leaving Swansea to paint or study music, while his father had cancer of the tongue, and his aunt Annie had just died. Fern Hill was no more for him, only Cwmdonkin Drive or a winter cottage at Blaen-Cwm, near Llangain, from where he wrote lengthily and sadly to his new London confidante, exchanging "insults and compliments, hasty judgements, wisdoms and nonsenses". Photographs were also exchanged, with Dylan finding Miss Johnson's appearance a little strong for him – he entitled her Wilhelmina. He professed himself indifferent to her accounts of her previous loves, although his little Welsh ear was open to all secrets. He recommended her to fasten her "affections on some immaculately profiled young man, and love the swine to death. Love among the angels is a perpetual distemper." In fact, the evidence and length of Dylan's correspondence shows him perfectly ready to love his Pamela without passing her off elsewhere, although it took him many letters to confess to that awakening.

Most interesting in the early letters to London is Dylan's need to reveal himself, or rather, to set himself down as he wished to be. He seems to have had an obsession about proving himself the coming poet, ribald and wise and doomed by death. He admits to being so far behind Blake "that only the wings of his heels are in sight." His search is for the one right word, for there is always one and only one. That is the poet's job, not politics. "There is no necessity for the artist to do anything . . . He is a law unto himself, and his greatness or smallness rises or falls by that." Dylan does not want to express what other people have felt, but "to rip something away and show what they have never seen." Simultaneously, he is scared of his appearance to the girl he has never met, asking her not to expect too much from "a thin, curly little person, smoking too many cigarettes, with a crocked lung, and writing his vague verses in the back room of a provincial villa."

Between his vaunting ambition as a poet and his personal insecurity, Dylan's letters to Pamela Hansford Johnson climb and slip. His method of composing them is careful enough, as if he meant them to be preserved as a record of the young dog in his Swansea days. He would jot down random ideas on pieces of paper, hoard them, arrange them, then copy them out in long letters under paragraph headings. Early on in the correspondence, there is a description of a Swansea day, the lazy bedwarming and smoking morning of newspapers and shaving and reading the latest periodicals and books, the walk to the pub before lunch at home, the afternoon walk on the Gower cliffs, tea and writing and evening pubs, and so to bed. Contrasted with this sloth, the same letter tells urgently of the seed of resolution inside every thinking man, of the mysteries of true poetry, of the country of the spirit called God, of the man who loves as one and the same with the man who hates, for "a blow can be a kiss out of heaven, and a kiss a blow out of hell."

Dylan's country cottage life shows an equal contrast between the ills of the flesh and the swoops of the spirit. At Blaen-Cwm, Dylan even found a bureau bearing a photograph of himself at the age of seven, "thick-lipped, Fauntleroy-haired, wide-eyed, and empty as the bureau itself." After a bus ride there through the industrial towns of South

Wales in the grey rain, Dylan protests that he has had enough of his own bloody country, that he wants "out of narrowness and dirtiness, out of the eternal ugliness of the Welsh people, and all that belongs to them." But in contrast to his depression, he later retires "like an emaciated Cupid with pen for arrow, to a bleak, unmaidened bed," there to write out, 'Thomas: HIS IDEAS'. These are his attacks on sexual convention and hypocrisy, containing perhaps a grain of hope for his future relationship with his Pamela; "the honest friendship of boy & girl" is to be allowed "entire freedom and culmination," without any agreement between their families; his is a dream of a society where boys and girls are free to have as many lovers as they wish until they find a lover with whom they can be for a longer time, or for ever. Such is Dylan's vision in constrained wet Wales, where he often feels "so utterly and suicidally morbid" that his letters should read like an excerpt from the *Undertakers' Gazette*.

Dylan's way out of Swansea is through voice as well as pen. He recommends to his poetess the speaking of her poems. He himself chants aloud in a sonorous voice every poem he reads. "The neighbours must know your poems by heart," he insists, "they certainly know my own, and are bound to be acquainted with many passages of Macbeth, Death's Jester, and the Prophetic Books. I often think that baths were built especially for drowsy poets to lie in and there intone aloud amid the steam and boiling ripples." He continues in his letters to write parodies of poems and mockeries of himself, and he begins to show a touching opening in the hedgehog points of the prickly young poet, saying how important to him is the freedom of his writing to her, and asking her forgiveness for his vulgarity and attacks on her poems. He promises not to run himself down any more; "by this time you know as many of my faults and shortcomings as I do myself." This is the first and last time he has ever written in confession and appreciation.

So Dylan moves, in the correspondence, from self-defence into self-mockery and on to a tentative trust. As he accuses her from her photograph of bristling with individuality, "images of a herd of porcupine", so he blunts his own quills. He finds her a terribly accomplished person, while he can't sing or play music or draw, and even his acting is only of madmen, neurotics, nasty modern young men and vulgar comedians. He cannot, however, give up his low style for her high style. He is damned if he will swap his "warmy wombs for all the fairy bubbles this side of St. Paul's. We're extremists, girl, one upstairs in our lady's chamber and the other downstairs in our lady's chamber-pot." He urges his Pamela not to be a successful neo-Georgian poet, but to follow her "selfspring; everything comes out of yourself, and darkness, despite what you say, has infinitely more possibilities than day." His own poetry is not facile, but written at the speed of two lines for each "painful, brain-racking and sweaty" hour. And as for present times, civilisation is the murderer, the coming revolution the hope, everything wrong that forbids the freedom of the individual.

So Dylan begins to take off the hard mackintosh of the tough youth around town and show himself as naked and vulnerable as he was. His letters to Miss Johnson begin with the urge to shock and outrage, and they end with the need to love and be loved. His criticism of D. H. Lawrence in them is most interesting. He attacks Lawrence for his paganism and sex-and-sun loving – something that had appealed to the seventeen-year-old Dylan and was now becoming meaningless. "A born writer is born scrofulous; his career is an accident dictated by physical or circumstantial disabilities." Lawrence was weak and diseased but insisted on writing of the struggle of the ideas of the pagan strong, thus making his writing "a *lie* from start to finish". Dylan now confesses that his own early defence of the body being all is unsatisfactory. The life of the body is terribly limited, while the life of the non-body is capable of realising infinity, of getting somewhere.

By giving up his defences, by admitting himself to himself in letters to another, Dylan does not claim to become free of his obsessions. In fact, he gloats over his complexes. They give him an "immense, if unholy, joy . . . like a dead man exulting in the company of his beetles." He tries staring at his friend Dan Jones across a room until optical distortion makes him see new features on the other's face, "the antlers of a deer, or a cloven foot, or the fingers of a hand, or a thing no words can ever describe, a shape, not beautiful or horrible, but as deep as hell and as quiet as heaven." It is an invoking of devils, and by God, they come. But from the dead flesh that obsesses the young Dylan, he will build up a living flesh through his faith. Some day, however, he will try to write "something altogether out of the hangman's sphere, something larger, wider, more comprehensible, and less selfcentred." One day he might even come up to her expectations.

So ended the year of 1933, with Dylan setting himself good resolutions. He will think nothing in the world ugly, not even the dung of a pig. He will not label the brain into separate compartments, differentiating between the poet in himself and the need to eat lunch. "It is said to be mad to write poetry and sane to lunch at one o'clock; but it is the other

Photograph of D. H. Lawrence on the wall of Dylan's toolshed in Laugharne.

way about." He wants to believe in dragons and a new colour, so much whiter than white that white is black. He wants to forget all that he has ever written and start again, "informed with a new wonder, empty of all my old dreariness, and rid of the sophistication which is disease." Above all, in the shape of a boy "and a funny boy at that," in the very short time he has left, Dylan wants "to live and love & be loved; I want to praise and be praised; I want to sleep and wake, and look upon my sleeping as only another waking; I want to live and die."

So in a few months of correspondence with someone he feels to be his equal and on the side of his angels, Dylan largely matures and gives up his posturings and rantings for a simplicity that is to inform and illuminate his best poetry. He feels himself free to confess himself and not feel condemned for it. He senses the surge of potential so strongly that it induces wonder rather than self-disdain. Above all, he no longer is alone in his sprawling, dreaming youthful ambitions. If he is not certain, if he never will be able to resolve the contradictions within his society and himself, yet he can hope now, "a short, ambiguous person in a runcible hat, feeling very lost in a big and magic universe," wishing his Pamela "love and a healthy new year."

The meeting between the two young poets, already half in love with each other and their own correspondence, took place in February 1934. Dylan was nineteen, Pamela Hansford Johnson was twenty-one, both were nervous. He arrived at her aunt's place in Battersea in a pork-pie hat, polo-necked sweater, and a raincoat with bulging pockets. He had prepared his opening remark. "It's nice to meet you after all those letters. Have you seen the Gauguins?" He stayed for a week on that visit to London, for six weeks on his next visit, and on and off during the following year, walking with his Pamela on Clapham Common or taking the bus to Chelsea, seeing a Sean O'Casey play and trying to get a literary job. His appearance, according to Miss Johnson, was very lovable.

> He revealed a large and remarkable head, not shaggy – for he was visiting – but heavy with hair the dull gold of threepenny bits springing in deep waves and curls from a precise middle parting. His brow was very broad, not very high: his eyes, the colour and opacity of caramels when he was solemn, the colour and transparency of sherry when he was lively, were large and fine, the lower rims rather heavily pigmented. His nose was a blob; his thick lips had a chapped appearance; a fleck of cigarette paper was stuck to the lower one. His chin was small, and the disparity between the breadth of the lower and upper parts of his face gave an impression at the same time comic and beautiful. He looked like a brilliant, audacious child, and at once my family loved and fussed over him as if he were one.

Although Dylan found no work to keep him in London and had to go home to Wales – seen off by Pamela in a mood of supreme depression – he soon wrote to her that he loved her. This letter and its successor have not been published, only a third one in which Dylan says he regrets his famous love letter with all the conviction of his murky conscience, also the pathos of the second folio. He promises now to "keep clear of the emotional element" even though he knows nothing can be spoilt between him and Pamela. He shows himself resilient and back to his old bad jokes. He also sees a future in London opening

55

before him, with letters from Stephen Spender arriving, and T. S. Eliot asking him to call, although he confesses to Pamela that he is "not half as brave, dogmatic & collected in the company of Literary persons" as he might have led her to believe. His recent poem in the *Listener* has even caused Sir John Reith and the British Broadcasting Corporation to print a public apology for its obscenity, particularly for the lines:

> A candle in the thighs
> Warms youth and seed and burns the seeds of age...

Dylan claims to Pamela that his poetry has now been banned from being broadcast, all for three other lines, not about copulation, but about a metaphysical image of rain and grief:

> Nor fenced, nor staked, the gushers of the sky
> Spout to the rod
> Divining in a smile the oil of tears.

Yet Pamela's luck along with her love had begun to rub off on Dylan. The *Sunday Referee* offered as its Poetry Prize the printing of a book of poems. Her work had been the first book printed; his work would be the second. The editorial staff of the newspaper felt that it was impossible for so young a man to write such extraordinary poetry and sent him his train fare, in order to see if he really was the author. They were satisfied, and Dylan spent the Easter of 1934 with Pamela and her family and a future opening out in front of him; he even attended his first literary lunch at the Café Royal. Both he and Pamela were preparing to write prose now, he his *Red Book* of short stories, she her first successful novel, *This Bed Their Centre*. Even back in Swansea, Dylan no longer felt beset by enemies on all sides, but safe in a ring of love, in the protection of Pamela's understanding. He only hated being solitary in his bedroom at home, like any young lover. "Why aren't you here with me, in my little circle, holding my hand & braving the wicked world with me? Don't tell me – I know. The world is so wickedly wicked it won't let you brave it with me."

Yet Dylan remained solitary and thin-skinned, living within his own pride, fierce and vulnerable, even fearful of his new love. "How horribly easy it is to be hurt," he writes to Pamela. "I am being hurt all day long & by the finest & most subtle things. So on goes the everyday armour, and the self, even the wounded self, is hidden from so many.

Opposite: *Portrait of Dylan Thomas by Augustus John.*

If I pull down the metals, don't shoot, dear." Yet he does pull down the metals to her in nearly every line. He writes that he believes they will live together one day "as happily as two lobsters in a saucepan, two bugs on a muscle, one smile, though never to vanish, on the Cheshire face," even if their idyll ends with Tax Collectors, him nuts and her gaga. But in the meantime, he needs an anti-mercenary job in London. He despairs that he is "as green as ever as to what I must do in this dull, grey country, & how one little colour must be made out of you and me."

An exile at home, Dylan polished his *18 Poems* throughout the early part of 1934, yearning for his "Pamela and a Chatterton attic". He found the writing of poetry very difficult now, complaining of working on six lines as hard as a navvy, only to find that he had picked and cleaned them of all except their barbaric sounds. He decided he was "a freak user of words, not a poet". He thought his lines abstruse and meaningless, not the words he wanted to express. In the end, he went away to stay at Laugharne with a new friend, Glyn Gower Jones, in "the strangest town in Wales".

At Laugharne, indeed, Dylan acted as if under a black spell. The whole mood of his letters changes. He writes of working as a Symbol Simon on a novel as ambitious as the Divine Comedy with a chorus of deadly sins, the incarnated figures of Love and Death, an Immaculate Conception, a bald-headed girl, a celestial tramp, a mock Christ, and the Holy Ghost. He himself feels tortured "by every doubt and mis-giving that an hereditarily twisted imagination, an hereditary thirst and a commercial quenching, a craving for a body not my own, a chequered education and too much egocentric poetry, and a wild, wet day in a tidied town, are capable of conjuring out of their helly deeps." He has lost faith in his work. "There is torture in words, torture in their linking & spelling, in the snail of their course on stolen paper, in their sound that the four winds double, and in my knowledge of their inadequacy." He agrees with Buddha that the essence of life is evil. It is a "hopeless, fallen angel of a day." And although Dylan ends the letter with protests of his love for Pamela and disclaimers of his rantings and rumblings, yet he sends the letter to show his black-dog mood that is to end in his deliberate destruction of his intellectual love-affair.

Dylan's next letter reveals his adolescent urge to swank and his puritan conscience; it contradicts the new maturity of his poems. He describes, in a prose so simple and a handwriting so bad that it seems to come straight from his sense of sin, a week-end in Gower with a reporter friend and his fiancée. All three got drunk, the girl left the friend to spend four nights in Dylan's bed, and everybody was swilling all the time. Dylan's confession continues, "Oh darling, it hurts me to tell you this but I've got to tell you because I always want to tell you the truth about me. And I never want to share. It's you & me or nobody, you and me and nobody. But I have been a bloody fool & I'm going to bed for a week. I'm just on the borders of D.T.'s darling and I've wasted some of my tremendous love for you on a lank, redmouthed girl with a reputation like a hell." So the outpouring of shame, mixed with pride, continues to the end of the letter, with a demand that he must come to London to be with his Pamela, if she will ever see him again.

Dylan so wallowed with guilty luxury in his sense of sin and manhood and truth at all costs, that he did not calculate on Pamela's reaction.

Left to right: *Pamela Hansford Johnson, Aunt Pollie, Mrs Thomas, Uncle Dai, Aunt Dosie Rees, Uncle Bob; Wales, 1936.*

Predictably, she was mortified, writing probably about this letter in her diary on the 27th of May, "Appalling distressing letter from Dylan. I cried lustily nearly all day and had to write telling him it must finish. So an end to that affair." It was not an end to that affair, since affairs of the mind as well as of the heart do not end like theatrical exits on a note of drama. Miss Johnson saw Dylan again on the 12th of June in London, when he stayed with her for two weeks. In her delight of getting him back and his delight of being forgiven, he pressed her to marry him, and she nearly accepted. But she had second thoughts, perhaps about the Gower episode, and the love affair was allowed to peter away in another visit of Dylan to London and in her visits to Wales to meet his family; there at last she saw the room where Dylan wrote most of his poems, and which he had described to her as "a tiny, renovated bedroom, all papers and books, cigarette ends, hardly any light. *Very* tiny. I really have to go out to turn around. Cut atmosphere

Dylan with Pamela Hansford Johnson in Wales in 1934.

with a book-knife. No red cushion. No cushion at all. Hard chair. Smelly. Painful. Hot water pipes very near. Gurgle all the time. Nearly go mad."

The visit to Wales was not a great success for Miss Johnson and her mother, who found the garrulous Mrs Thomas rather tiresome. Dylan's true age came out, a mere nineteen years old, and Miss Johnson began to realise the impossibility of the situation. Fairly conventional herself, she would not live with Dylan before marriage, and he was too young to marry and too sexually pressing to wait. His demands on her had become urgent since the Gower escapade and had led to appalling rows on his last trip to London, where he had often spent the August nights drinking in order not to come back sober to the same house where his unattainable love was sleeping. In modern times, the sexual and social barriers between Dylan and his Pamela might have been lifted with ease; but the age of permissive families was decades away from the relationship of Mr Thomas from Cwmdonkin Drive and Miss Johnson from Battersea.

So the relationship ended in the normal formal letter, which explained nothing, and yet had to be written. It is dated Spring, 1935. Dylan wrote: "I should have written what's much too long a time ago, because there's so much to explain and so much that, perhaps, will, and should, never be explained – it means such a lot of belly rubbing and really tearful apologies on my blasted part. But never mind that. Britons never will be slaves, and I'm a rat."

He was not. He had merely gone through a first great love, and he had shown the contradictions of his nature and of his society. He adored the free love of an intellectual affair with a poetess; but the free love of their bodies was impossible in the suburban surroundings of the depression years. He enjoyed the pleasures and remorses of his drunken week-end with the loose red-mouthed girl in Gower; yet his primary sense of Welsh sin, his elementary vision of a hell of poisoned drink and Jezebels, sent him to the confessional and half-way to the registry office with his Pamela within three weeks. He was liberated by finding out that he was acceptable and lovable to the young poets of London; but he was bound by the provincial and middle-class necessity to earn enough money to set himself up in London, if he wanted to live there with his respectable love. He could never escape the warm spoiling of his youth, the safe fug of his "womb with a view" onto a wall and the far Welsh sea. He was too young to look after himself, let alone another. Only his poetry denied his lack of years.

From Chelsea to Donegal

This is the quarter of the pseudo-artists, of the beards, of the naughty expressions of an entirely outmoded period of artistic importance and of the most boring Bohemian parties I have ever thought possible.

Slightly drunk, slightly dirty, slightly wicked, slightly crazed, we repeat our platitudes on Gauguin and Van Gogh as though they were the most original things in the world. There are, of course, scores of better people that I do meet, but these little maggots are my companions for most of the time. I think I shall change my digs quite soon.

from a letter to Bert Trick by Dylan Thomas, December, 1934

Opposite: *Portrait of Mervyn Levy by Alfred Janes.*

63

From Chelsea to Donegal

In *Adventures in the Skin Trade*, Sam Bennet spoiled his father's examination papers and dirtied his parents' house in Swansea before running away to sinful London. In actual fact, Dylan left with his father's blessing and his friend Fred Janes in a car in November, 1934, to begin his independent life off the Fulham Road on the borders of Chelsea in a large room in Redcliffe Street. Here he found it hard to work in such muddled and messy surroundings. For yards around him, he could "see nothing but poems, poems, poems, butter, eggs, mashed potatoes, mashed among my stories and Janes' canvases. One day we shall have to wash up, and then perhaps I can really begin to work." Winter conditions did not improve his outlook or output. By February, he was excusing his lateness in replying to a letter, because of

> the abominable cold cramping the fingers, elongating the sweet hours of bed, and forcing, eventually, the tired half sleeper to erect a small fire in an insufficient grate; the skin of laziness, cancelling the positive virtue that regards sin and virtue lazily, equally and equably; the lack of ink . . . ; the worries of a life that consists, for the most part, in building the brain on paper and pulling down the body, the small and too weak body to stand either the erection of a proper brain or the rubbing of saloon counters: the pressure of words, the lack of stamps; flu in embryo . . .

Coming to London had the virtue of making Dylan Thomas better known to the London poets and editors, and the vice of making it hard for him to do more than hack-work, reviewing books. The condition of his future life already began to be formed on this first independent stay, the excitement of the city leading to a physical collapse that sent

Opposite: *The last view of Swansea.*

him away to the convalescence of Wales, where he would write poetry and become bored to death. Certainly, his reviews in the London literary magazines show little depth and much invective. The provincial bombard thunders overmuch. Stephen Spender is accused of lines, passages, and clusters of images of an uncommon facility and ugliness. Thomas Moult, the unfortunate editor of *The Best Poems of 1934*, is dressed down for selecting the worst poems of the year. Anthologies are, anyway, "pernicious to the intelligent reading of poetry; one poem sucks the blood of another; two or more similar varieties of talent are apt to cancel out." As for two books of verse by two young men, actually Lyle Donaghy and John Lehmann, Dylan starts his review with the line: "It can be said, with the utmost sympathy, that a poet should have his bottom kicked every week." As a young reviewer, this might more aptly have been done to the bumptious Dylan, so vulnerable to criticism of his own poetry.

In fact, the slim volume of Dylan's *18 Poems* was fortunate in its reception, receiving praise from Rayner Heppenstall, Edwin Muir, and finally from Edith Sitwell, whom Dylan had recently called in a private letter "a poisonous thing of a woman" who wrote "virgin dung". This first book of Dylan's was actually published on the 18th of December, 1934, in an edition of five hundred copies, some of the cost provided by an avant-garde bookshop run by David Archer, a young man in revolt from his public-school and Cambridge values. Dylan was becoming a little known, mainly due to the championship of Stephen Spender. Even those who were wary of him and whom he often disliked, such as Geoffrey Grigson, the editor of *New Verse*, befriended his talent without accepting his nature. Grigson's account of him in 1934 is most revealing, stating that Dylan had not yet sloughed off enough of lowest-middle-class Swansea. "He was not so cocky. He needed assurance with which he was never generously and liberally supplied . . ." He was uncertain of the part he was acting, the Rossetti angel-poet or Rimbaud. His features were "still unpoached at this time." But London quickly intimidated Dylan less, was entered by him more, until he soon found that it "preferred to aesthetic debauch, or its uniform, the Toughish Boy, the Boy with a Load o'Beer, in and out, so boringly, of the pubs."

Constantine Fitzgibbon, Dylan's admirable biographer, goes at length into the reasons for Dylan's continual drunkenness. Some were psychological; he simply had no head for drink and became drunk far too easily. Some lay in his Welsh background; drunkenness was a denial of his Welsh chapel education. Another cause for drinking was his insomnia; as he wrote in one letter to Miss Johnson, at times he did not sleep for a fortnight and tried everything, pills and counting sheep, getting drunk and staying sober, but nothing worked. Dylan was not, indeed, an alcoholic. He did not crave drink, only the ease which it brought to his overworking brain and the facile company that relieved his solitude. As Fitzgibbon testifies, Dylan went for weeks of his life only drinking weak tea for enjoyment, and he was no more of a true alcoholic than an outgoing woman may be a true nymphomaniac. "Dylan drank as a woman may be promiscuous, for many of the same reasons."

Dylan's promiscuity, during these first London years after his drift from Miss Johnson and before his meeting with Caitlin Macnamara, was also more casual than lustful, more for company than for sensation, more passive than active. Fitzgibbon again suggests that Dylan seldom, if ever, went to bed with women before his marriage, except if he had been drinking. He was continually short of sleeping-places near to his pubs, and he would find himself in a convenient bed more often than a chosen one. If his life at the time was like Captain Cat's sea-life "sardined with women", yet he could complain to Rayner Heppenstall one night as he sidled along to Bloomsbury and his probable fate, "Oh God, I'm so tired of sleeping with women I don't even like." Many writers are bad at being promiscuous with women, from the certainty of knowing how the affair will end before it has even begun. After the deprivations of his Swansea youth, Dylan was often too weak to resist an opportunity in the glad-eyed pubs of London; but his enjoyment was always tempered by his sense of waste.

Once the first desperate denial of the Welsh chapel was over, the final reason of Dylan's generous exposure of himself to drink and women in London seems to have been more through timidity than aggression, more through acceptance than attack. In *Adventures in the Skin Trade*, he gives his young Welsh hero Sam Bennet the curious quality of attracting adventures to him by accepting life in every position, "like a baby who had been given self-dependence." People would come to Sam Bennet, bringing life, and he would go on. As Dylan once said, when asked why he drank too much, "Because they expect it of me."

Dylan's defence of himself in his novel as an innocent and his accusation of others as the inveiglers might not have been totally true, but it was partially so. Dylan was too lazy and too passive to resist temptation, particularly in London pubs; there he found social convention egged him on to excess, whereas small-town Wales had haltered him. His trouble was to find a balance and a moderation, which he never did. And if his role of the *enfant terrible* was essentially false, yet he played it to its death and his own.

Richard Burton has described one other seduction in Dylan's drinking. While every man who met him loved the extraordinary warmth of his natural personality and wit, Burton has said that Dylan was only the most magical and wittiest spell-binder in the world between the third and the eighth drink. Before that, he was morose. After that, he was uproarious or maudlin. But in that middle ground of alcohol, that every man's land of gab, when his fears and inhibitions were gone, the actor met the poet in a riot of fancy and words.

Dylan's early ménage with Fred Janes was soon joined by a third friend from Swansea, Mervyn Levy, in a new bare room nearer the transplanted heart of Chelsea – as Dylan once objected, "this bloody land is full of Welshmen." Levy played the bohemian artist, while Janes played the serious one, even collecting Dylan's rent by holding Dylan's trousers (with him inside them or not) upside down until the coins fell out on the floor. Levy liked playing the clown, Groucho Marx to Dylan's Harpo – a role which Dylan could play very well with his halo of yellow curls and eyes full of innocence and deceit. Levy encouraged the fantastical vein in Dylan as well as begging on the pavement for beers, if necessary. As he wrote, "Wandering the streets . . . we wove incredible fantasies as we so often did when we were together for a while. How many mice would it take to pull the London to Glasgow Express? Half a million? A million? Oh! More, lots more! Don't forget they'd have to pull it at the same speed as it normally goes. Anyway, if you had *enough* mice you could do it. It stood to reason."

This was the time that Dylan was more waif and stray than plump and bully. It was the period of the famous Augustus John painting of him which hangs in Cardiff. This was described by Dylan as "that dewy goblin portrait frog-goggling . . . out of the past." In the memoirs of the London bohemians of the 1930s, indeed, Dylan does wander on and off like a Robin Goodfellow. To the poet George Barker, he was small and thin, with a dirty wool scarf wound around himself like an old love affair, looking like a runaway schoolboy. To the impressionable Sheila MacLeod, he was "a handsome cherubic youth, crowned with an aura of thunderous power and doom." To another observer of the

Opposite: *Richard Burton by the Druid stones overlooking Fishguard, where Dylan had visualised the dawn-sequence in* Under Milk Wood.

young poets who clustered around the Archer bookshop, "young though he was, he seemed old: a strange grubby figure, dressed in a skimpy, green sweater, with tousled hair and bitten nails", a forerunner of the Angry Young Men. "Some of his admirers likened him to Chatterton. Others expected him to commit suicide quite soon; his enemies described him as a boor."

Such was the London face that Dylan showed in his first long stay there. He could get away with any excesses, because he appeared elfin and his work was promising. But as A. E. Ellis has declared, nothing is further from performance than promise. Dylan found that London was not a place to work in, only to fritter and bluster away his talent for words. At the beginning of March, 1935, he was back in Swansea, writing to Glyn Jones that the trials of his life had proved too much for him, the courts had found him guilty, and that he had come home for a few weeks, rather hollow-eyed and with little real work to his credit. He had to get to the country to get on with his poems. Even Swansea, especially Swansea, was no womb now, for the few old friends who remained had jobs and marriages, and the writing Dylan had no time for too much beer in the evenings – "at least temporarily".

So Dylan left soon for the ultimate seclusion, a cottage in Donegal converted by Rockwell Kent into a studio. Despite their caginess towards each other, Dylan met with Geoffrey Grigson, for his first week there. Grigson described him as the Swansea Changeling, translated to the side of an Irish "cold, soul-tightening ocean", chanting "We are the Dead" to the echoes reverberating "We are the Dead, the Dead, the Dead, the Dead." Peat fires and potheen, potatoes and buttermilk healed Dylan on his own, once Grigson had gone. The poet described his impressions to Bert Trick, saying he was as lonely as Christ sometimes in a poor, dirty land, where "the pigs rut and scrabble in the parlours," and the people were superstitious or mad, whining or boring, and the blood sports were blood sports. Naturally, the West Coast of Ireland was beautiful and wild, but it could not cure Dylan's restlessness. Like the swallow in the hall of the Old English poem, *The Wanderer*, Dylan felt he had to pass on, even if he was to come back to Wales. "I wouldn't be at home if I were at home. Everywhere I find myself seems to be nothing but a resting place between places that become resting places between resting places themselves . . . the body and the brain, all the centres of movement, must shift or die. It may be a primary loneliness that makes me out-of-home. It may be this or that, and this or that is enough for today. Poor Dylan. Poor him. Poor me."

If Dylan was full of self-pity about the intolerable essence of his craft, the solitude needed to write poems, he was perfectly inconsequential about his method of escape. Having announced that he would stay until September, he walked off early over the hills and far away without paying his bills to the local farmer and his wife, who had looked after him. One of Dylan's friends finally settled the matter, but Dylan was merely pouting and unrepentant, "acting the injured Suckling."

These were the repetitive extremes of Dylan's life, the interminable reactions of his later days. Excess in the city sent him off to boredom in the country. After a little rural work at words, he had to scuttle back to the city, leaving his peace and his bills behind him. As he wrote at the end of 1935, he had spent most of the summer in Donegal and had done a lot of good work there, but "a wave of rather alcoholic laziness" had set in since at home in Swansea, and he was only just beginning to put words together again. "The poetry machine is so well oiled now it should work without a hitch until my next intellectually ruinous visit to the bowels of London." Poor Dylan. Poor him.

Pencil-drawing of Dylan by Mervyn Levy.

Adventures in the Skin Trade

I'm not a country man; I stand for, if anything, the aspidistra, the provincial drive, the morning café, the evening pub; I'd like to believe in the wide open spaces as the wrapping around walls, the windy boredom between house and house, hotel and cinema, bookshop and tube-station; man made his house to keep the world and the weather out, making his own weathery world inside; that's the trouble with the country: there's too much public world between the private ones.

from a letter to Vernon Watkins by Dylan Thomas, 20th April, 1936

Back view of Dylan's boyhood home in Swansea.

Adventures in the Skin Trade

Dylan's illusion all his life was that he had rejected suburban values completely. This was not true. In 1936, he spent much of his time in Swansea and began to recognise his affection for a place that he had never really rejected, except in his fantasies. During 1936, he did actually admit to his new friend Vernon Watkins that he stood for, if anything, the aspidistra and the provincial drive. But this was still an admission only to intimates. For public consumption, he was the Swansea rebel, who could not wait to get away.

This self-delusion of Dylan's is strongest in his unfinished work, *Adventures in the Skin Trade*. Although it was not written until the first years of the war, and although it was set down after his loving memories of Swansea collected in *Portrait of the Artist as a Young Dog*, it represents the full imaginative rebellion of Dylan from his secure childhood and youth, swaddled by villas. As Vernon Watkins explains, *Adventures in the Skin Trade* was meant by Dylan to be "an extended story, not strictly autobiographical, but bearing a relation to the two parts of his experience, his own actions and the actions of his dramatised self." The hero would actually do what Dylan dreamed of doing and never did; he would make a total break with the past before taking the same train to unknown London which Dylan had actually once taken.

In its conception, the novel was ambitious. Dylan intended his passive young hero, Sam Bennet, to lose each of his seven skins to one of the seven deadly sins until finally Sam would be left naked, after a comic journey through the circles of the Inferno of London. In a short piece entitled 'Prologue to an Adventure', published in the first number of *Wales* in the summer of 1937, Dylan's thoughts of flaying London were already beginning to form. His narrator was himself, walking through the wilderness of this world, the strange city of a "mister lonely", beckoned by "ladies on their own, ... naked as new-born mice".

Heaven and hell shift up and down that city: and the night-club he enters is explicitly called the Seven Sins. There two little girls dance bare-foot in the sawdust, and a bottle splinters on their legs. A negress kisses him, but he escapes into the night and the rocking city, where "the seven deadly sins wait tidelessly for the moon." Now he goes in at the door of the Deadly Virtues, where the sea of faces parts, and he stumbles forward to the fiery bottles. "Brandy for the dreamer", a wooden voice says, and he gets drunk before lurching out again into a city where the pavements are mazes dragging down the drinkers from a world of light into a crawling sea-bed.

This sketch for the later novel is worth examining because its obsessive themes remain in the structure of *Adventures in the Skin Trade*. By 1941, when Dylan was actually writing the opening chapters, he dismissed his intentions as merely "a mixture of Oliver Twist, Little Dorrit, Kafka, Beachcomber, and good old 3-adjectives-a-penny belly-churning Thomas, the Rimbaud of Cwmdonkin Drive." He wrote the first three chapters of the novel quickly, carried along by the comic fantasy and anarchy of its surface, almost unconscious of its obsessive basis. Vernon Watkins thinks that he abandoned the novel half-done because the greater and crueller anarchy of the war, which distorted London beyond measure, took the place of his nightmare city. The black-out made London even more of a pit than Dylan's imagination could dig for it. In fact, the novel stopped because Dylan became a screen-writer later that year, and somehow he never got back to his fragment, even though he was trying to continue the novel as late as the year before he died.

The first obsession of the novel is escape, the break with Swansea. Sam Bennet silently and ineffectively destroys his parents' home in Mortimer Street, off Stanley's Grove, with his eyes still heavy from a dream of untouchable city women. He wants to cause so much destruction that he will never be *allowed* to come back home again. Fearing his own ignorant, lazy, dishonest and sentimental character, easily influenced by anybody, he wishes to prevent himself from returning by an unforgivable act of wanton destruction. So, when his family see him off to the train – still unaware of the minor havoc in Mortimer Street – Sam Bennet can turn for a last look and see "three strangers waving". He has cut his family wholly from his future. Dylan in his fantasy wanted to escape completely from Swansea; but he never did, and never could.

The second obsession of the novel is the total acceptance of the

Vernon Watkins on the Gower peninsula.

world and the refusal to manipulate one's own life. Dylan, in fact, used his contacts with poets and editors of poetry magazines to further his career; but Sam Bennet's first act in the train lavatory is to flush away the helping names, the influential numbers, the addresses that could mean so much in London. Sam only keeps his money and the number of an unknown girl. His first act on arrival is to sit in the railway buffet and have a beer, although, sadly enough, Swansea is already there in the person of the insufferable Ron Bishop, also up in the smoke. But Sam accepts the encounter with Mr Allingham, the furniture dealer, only too ready to help drink away the money of any new arrival, rattling

76

his fortune, fresh as Copperfield, straws in his hair. It is Sam's belief that something will happen, must happen to him, which finally annoys Mr Allingham into shifting him from the buffet with a bottle stuck onto his finger. Sam has to "give London a chance".

The third obsession shown in the novel is Dylan's love of a secure and overstuffed disorder. His own bedroom in Cwmdonkin Drive was a ragbag of clutter, while Mr Allingham's room is a pyramid of unsalable junk – and the best room Sam has ever seen. People disappear in the fullest room in England. They remain lost and easy and safe. Anyone can do anything in the room, nobody can see anyone. The perfect anarchic world.

At the High-Class tobacco shop, however, Dylan's fear of strict female authority has surfaced, the terror of the cruel and precise women that were to rule Dylan's pages, from Mrs Dacey with her head so prim that it might spill to Mrs Ogmore-Pritchard who shoo'd away the old sun for fear it might spoil the polish. In these comic gorgons, there is always a suppressed lust that is even more terrifying than their schoolmistress morality. Mrs Dacey mothers the fainting Sam about the hair and the mouth, while creaking like a door; she is all lechery and fingers cold as lizards; her hand aches on his thigh, five dry fishes drying on a cloth. The chapel dress on the bawd, the holy face fronting the suppressed desire, these Welsh habits clung to some of Dylan's own actions as well as informing his perceptions.

In Sam's bath scene with Mrs Dacey's daughter, Polly, Dylan's sexual passivity is revealed. Sam is conned by Polly into stripping naked and getting into an ice-cold bath in the dark. Polly says she is undressing; but she does not. She feeds him *eau de cologne* instead of brandy, knocks him out while she disappears. So the simple provincial is made bare and broken by the promises of loose city women, while he actually gets no sex and a split head for his trouble. Above all, Sam does not choose debauchery; its deceitful disaster inflicts itself upon him.

Now Sam Bennet reaches the fundamental obsessions shown in 'Prologue to an Adventure'. Mr Allingham, Mrs Dacey, and the homosexual George Ring take him on an infernal drunken plunge into the dives of London in a chapter headed 'Four Lost Souls'. They dance in the rain in the wet Edgware Road; they drink in a bar called the Antelope where they talk fiercely of sex; they take a taxi to the West End to call at the Gayspot, which is like a coal cellar, the bottom of the pit. "This was a breath and a scar of the London he had come to catch.

Look at the knickerless women enamouring from the cane tables,
waiting in the fumes for the country cousins to stagger in, all savings
and haywisps, or the rosy-cheeked old men with buttonholes whose
wives at home were as lively as bags of sprouts." But then the women
speak and disillusion sets in. Pub talk is pub talk anywhere. "London
is not under the bedclothes where all the company is grand and vile by a
flick of the cinema eye, and the warm linen doors are always open."
The knickerless women, first seen as enamouring shapes, were really
"dull as sisters, red-eyed and thick in the head with colds; they would
sneeze when you kissed them or hiccup and say Manners in the dark
traps of the hotel bedrooms." The way to hell was still paved with good
conventions.

The dive into the semi-depths ends with a fracas in the Gayspot,
with a bounce out onto the pouring pavements, and a final plunge into
the Cheerioh, which is indeed the ocean bed of London. There the
drinkers and dancers are the older brothers and sisters of those in the
Gayspot. "There were deep green faces, dipped in a sea dye, with
painted cockles for mouths and lichenous hair, sealed on the cheeks;
red and purple, slate-grey, tide-marked, rat-brown . . ." They are, as
Mr Allingham says, "the foul salt of the earth." And on this profound
and briney observation, *Adventures in the Skin Trade* comes to an
unfinished end, half-deep in the bowels of the infernal tides of London.

The reasons why Dylan never finished his comic novel are many.
Factually, the war and script-writing intervened; psychologically,
Dylan lost over the years the fine salacious wonder of the Swansea
Youth meeting the first shock of London – he had been there too often
by the time he tried to complete the novel in 1953. Also Dylan despised
his comic writing, however serious it was at base, for being done with
relative ease and interfering with the hard drafting of his poetry. Not
until the critical success of *Under Milk Wood* in his dying days could
Dylan rate his prose as highly as his verse. Humorous writing was a
paying and enjoyable interlude, not his craft or sullen art.

There is a deeper reason for *Adventures in the Skin Trade* remaining
unfinished. Dylan was perhaps too young and unaware in 1941 to
chronicle his own self-destruction in London. Although his poetry
throughout is permeated with the wish for death and the love of death,
it is still poetry. A factual, even if amusing, description of a disintegration
of a fantasy self through the seven deadly sins may need a certain
detachment from the process, in which Dylan was far too involved.
The same letter to Vernon Watkins in 1936, in which Dylan declared

himself a man of the aspidistra, also boasted that he had been in London for over a week, "and the same things happened there that always happen: I kept roughly a half of my appointments, met half the people I wanted to, met lots of other people, desirable and otherwise, and fully lived up to the conventions of Life No. 13: promiscuity, booze, coloured shirts, too much talk, too little work." There was an involvement with the city, which was inescapable and slowly fatal to Dylan. He could mock that involvement and describe it, but he could not end it nor describe his end from it.

Adventures in the Skin Trade is always fresh because provincial boys are always arriving in the "capital punishment" of the great city, expecting signals and wonders and debauches, and finding wet pavements and insecurity and disillusion. Another Welsh writer who arrived in London at much the same time as Dylan, Gwyn Thomas, has also described his first impressions, so similar to Sam Bennet's.

"The minute I got off the train my feet seemed to be perched on rolling boulders. And I have never landed there since without a sense of malignant insecurity. My mood has always been that of the man in whose wake I once left the station. He was walking up the ramp that leads into Praed Street. He was with his wife. He was lugging a large, scuffed suitcase. There was a look of crumpled innocence about them both. She was looking around her edgily, without gladness. He pointed at a newspaper poster. It said: *Nude Blonde Found Strangled In Paddington.*

"'See?' said the man. 'They're at it all the time.'"

Whatever he boasted, however much Dylan seemed a fish in the London depths, or indeed a chicken in a country Eden, he was always in his nature the boy from the Uplands, safe only in Swansea, whose adventures in the skin trade might result in the stripping of his skins by the deadly sins, but who would always grow those skins again as a defence of his own private world, in the way that the villas of the suburbs put on fresh coats of paint each spring to keep up with the Joneses.

Soho and Surrealism

The word is too much with us. He raised his pencil so that its shadow fell, a tower of wood and lead, on the clean paper; he fingered the pencil tower, the half-moon of his thumb-nail rising and setting behind the leaden spire. The tower fell, down fell the city of words, the walls of a poem, the symmetrical letters.

from 'The Orchards' DYLAN THOMAS

Opposite: *The 'French' pub in Dean Street, Soho.*

Soho and Surrealism

Oxford Street divides Soho into two parts. To the south, the restaurants and delicatessens and the film world and the last pub that is still as Dylan knew it, the "French" in Dean Street owned by Victor Berlemont, which still has its prints of boxers and actors all over the walls and its glass monument for dripping water into four Pernods all at once. To the north lies Fitzrovia on either side of Charlotte Street, a more secluded area of restaurants and food shops, where Dylan's favourite haunt was the Fitzroy Tavern, then run by a huge Russian called Kleinfeld, known occasionally for allowing credit on drinks. As Dylan's fellow-drinker and biographer Constantine Fitzgibbon has pointed out, the pubs were frequented by the writers and artists of the 1930s both because of economics and because of the need of petty bourgeois intellectuals to seem proletarian. Philip O'Connor has identified the Fitzrovia of the time as a national social garbage centre, where the poor artists were recruited from the suburban agony of the lower middle-class. "The charms of the district were those of minimal effort, of paddling in sensations wafted in by the busy proper people surrounding our encampment."

Out of licensing hours, there were the drinking clubs, which proliferated within the letter of the law in the interval of four hours between the noon and the evening pubs. There Dylan and his friends would booze away the lost afternoons, just as they would drink away the midnights in the old Café Royal, the nearest thing to a French café in London with its marble-topped tables and symbolic sandwiches. If anyone was in the money, the Gargoyle with its Matisse glass murals was the usual late-night haunt. But there were others, many others. . . .

Caitlin Macnamara, who was later to marry Dylan, lived much the same bohemian youth, since that old bohemian Augustus John was her neighbour in England. In her *Not Quite Posthumous Letter To My Daughter*, she tells of that frivolous age of the talented and creative young of the 1930s, with its "trivially crazy idea that it was *clever* to drink to extinction; and *clever* to be promiscuous to dulling the discrimination of the flesh." Anyone who did not join in these clever pastimes was considered drab and boring. Later on in life, Caitlin lamented that she was hypnotised by these commands to do wrong, that she had never raised herself by as much as an aspidistra or a potted palm into the enviable ranks of accepted uniformity.

The trouble was the old romantic and decadent notion that every orgy of excess was permitted to the Artist. In fact, in Caitlin's opinion, Dylan had a longer life than he might have had, because of his poverty and relative lack of fame in his early days. Success, and early success, was the tomb of the writer. "Luckily to Dylan the tomb came late, and he solved the issue of integrity quite simply; whenever in town, and confronted by the easier joys of telling endless stories to buddies in pubs from morning till night, by not working at all until he was back in the penitence of the country."

Such was the Soho and Fitzrovia background of Dylan's drinking days for twenty years, from the first time he came to London until the keg-of-bitter end. He never escaped his simple pleasure at the wickedness of London compared with Swansea or Laugharne. He knew it was a fraudulent wickedness, froth on the same old brew. Yet the city was bigger and the conversation was better and the big names more exciting. And there were his literary cronies, Norman Cameron and Oswell Blakeston, Geoffrey Grigson and William Empson, Rayner Heppenstall and Ruthven Todd, as well as his personal companions, Fred Janes and Mervyn Levy and William Scott, in whose rooms he would sleep on a mattress on the floor, never possessing even a room of his own. Soho and Fitzrovia were to Dylan a state of mind, with companions without boundaries, the escape from any need to do more than beg money and entertain. As he wrote in apology to a critic he had failed to see in 1936, "When I do come to town, bang go my plans in a horrid alcoholic explosion that scatters all my good intentions like bits of limbs and clothes over the doorsteps and into the saloon bars of the tawdriest pubs in London."

Yet London did provide for the young Dylan one of his more intense influences, from which he also had to escape – Surrealism. The obscurity of his earlier poems, the strange and intense juxtaposition of adjective and noun, and the violence of the imagery, made many critics confuse Dylan's youthful work with that of English Surrealist poets like David Gascoyne. The first and most important of these was Richard Church,

who was the poetry editor at J. M. Dent and Sons, and who had agreed to publish Dylan's second book of verse, his *Twenty-five Poems*. Church was a poet himself, who preferred Dylan's simpler efforts and criticised him for the Surrealism of his current and more obscure poems, stating that he had been "caught up in the delirium of intellectual fashion of the moment."

This Dylan denied, since many of the poems had originated in his earlier *Notebooks*. He wrote back on the 9th of December, 1935, that he had very little idea what Surrealism was and had never even read a page of Surrealist literature. Anyway, his poems were not Surrealist. A friend of his had replied to his enquiry, saying that Surrealist writing need not have any meaning at all. And while his own writing did suffer from "Immature violence, rhythmic monotony, frequent muddle-headedness, and a very much overweighted imagery," every line was meant to be understood. The reader was meant to understand every poem "by thinking and feeling about it, and not by sucking it in through his pores, or whatever he is meant to do with surrealist writing." Anyway, Dylan hoped in a later letter to Church that an understanding of him would not be confined to his simpler poems, and that the day might come when none of his poems would be "indecently obscure or fashionably difficult."

Richard Church did accept the poems for publication in September, 1936, and Dylan did become caught up in the latest intellectual fashion. He went to the Surrealist Exhibition held in the New Burlington Galleries in the June of that year. Although Dadaism and André Breton, Salvador Dali and Paul Eluard had become commonplace in smart Paris, they were hardly known in London. The attack of Surrealism on established values in art was still shocking across the Channel. And to a provincial youth like Dylan, this international subversion of all artistic traditions made his own defiance of conventions look no more important than a dog lifting its leg against a lamp-post.

At the Exhibition itself, which Dali attended in a deep-sea diver's suit, Dylan is said to have handed out boiled string in cups, inquiring politely, "Weak or strong?" As a young and rebellious poet, the richer circles of the Surrealists took him up briefly; he could be guaranteed in his role as an *enfant terrible* to add to the sensationalism of the moment. His biographer Fitzgibbon states that the Surrealist Exhibition led to Dylan's final débâcle before his marriage. He had been introduced to a

Opposite: *Drawing of Dylan by Mervyn Levy, 1947.*

Henry Treece

call-girl at a private view, who wore over her face a wire cage covered
entirely with roses. Later at her Mayfair house, Dylan caught a venereal
disease. The treatment for it was long and painful in the days before
penicillin, and the illness only encouraged Dylan's sense of sin and
pricked his conscience. It was in this mood that he first wrote to Caitlin
Macnamara that he loved her. He also had to give up alcohol during the
cure, and the effect on him was melancholy.

Yet if Dylan's physical brush with the international Surrealists was painful, yet their influence on his prose for four years was undeniable. Some of Dylan's stories were being published in Roger Roughton's Surrealist magazine, *Contemporary Poets and Prose*, and they were also to be published in his next work to be printed, *The Map of Love*. While the stories of this period have occasional images of power such as "night came down, hand on thigh", they are dense and clotted, full of mysticism and lack of clarity, violence and a striving for the unusual. There are intimations of themes to come in some of the stories, particularly in suggestions for the future Captain Cat of 'In the Direction of the Beginning', lines such as "he was a shoreman in deep sea, lashed by his hair to the eye in the cyclop breast, with his swept thighs strung among her voice; white bears swam and sailors drowned to the music she scaled and drew with hands and fables from his upright hair. . . ." Yet none of the stories succeed in themselves; they are knotted in their own webs of words, unlike the poems of that period, which are not wilfully obscure, but "a string of words stringed on a beanstick".

The stories do, however, link Dylan to his bardic roots, although the Surrealist techniques of the prose are not disciplined or clear enough to create a popular myth. In 'The Orchards', the hero's name is significantly Marlais, Dylan's own middle name, taken from the bardic name of his great-uncle. In the tale, the hero "sharpened his pencil and shut the sky out, shook back his untidy hair, arranged the papers of a devilish story on his desk, and broke the pencil-point with a too-hard scribble of 'sea' and 'fire' on a clean page. Fire would not set the ruled lines alight . . . nor water close over the bogy heads and the unwritten words. The story was dead from the devil up."

So it was. No incantation of complex prose could make the druidic pages blaze in Dylan's surreal period, except perhaps in 'The Burning Baby', which is the best of the overcharged efforts of this time. Basing himself on the true history of Doctor Price of Llantrisant, a self-declared druid and the apostle of cremation, Dylan wrote of this costumed old man burning the body of his dead illegitimate baby on the top of a hill at Caerlan. Dylan distorts the truth to make the baby incestuous, conceived of the old man's daughter, while the old man himself is changed to the vicar Rhys Rhys in order to shock opinion still more. In his sermons, the vicar preaches of the sins of the flesh and prays to God in the image of our flesh. Later "merry with desire, Rhys Rhys cast the bible on the floor."

Dylan's early prose suffered not only from the obscurities of Surrealism, but from the need to offend gratuitously. In addition, his overt concentration on Welsh myth rather than on the Welsh present and people makes these first stories somewhat unreadable. Richard Church may have been wrong in criticising Dylan's early poems for the influence of Surrealism, but he certainly seems to have put Dylan's prose on the right path. He suggested that Dylan write stories about his original world of Swansea, something that Dylan was to do in his first successful prose writing, the stories collected in *Portrait of the Artist as a Young Dog*. These stories did, indeed, put an end to the surreal fever in Dylan's prose of the late thirties and get him finally to work on what he had promised Church, a Welsh idea which "would clear up nearly all the vaguenesses and leave me something practical and (almost) commercial to work upon."

Throughout this period, a poet and critic called Henry Treece was working on the first major evaluation of Dylan's poetry. Treece began his study with a defence of Dylan from the charge of being a Surrealist poet. He compared poems of Dylan's with those of David Gascoyne, but he proved fairly conclusively that Dylan's images came from the subconscious controlled by logic rather than from the spontaneous subconscious. To Treece, a Surrealist line such as "the strident crying of red eggs" had little value beside wrought lines of Dylan's such as:

> Which is the world? Of our two sleepings, which
> Shall fall awake when cures and their itch
> Raise up this red-eyed earth?

In his letters to Treece, Dylan thanked him for his defence and praised him for his critical method. Treece's lucid comparisons convinced Dylan once again that "my own sane bee in the bonnet can never be a pal of that French wasp forever stinging itself to a loud and undignified death with a tail of boiled string." Dylan had recovered from his fashionable bath in claptrap and clap. At the end of his life, he could defend himself trenchantly against the influence of the Surrealists, stating his profound disagreement with their creed. "To them, chaos is the shape and order. This seems to me to be exceedingly presumptuous; the Surrealists imagine that whatever they dredge from their subconscious selves and put down in paint or in words must, essentially, be of some interest or value. I deny this."

A reading of the forty-three of Dylan's poems collected in book form and printed in 1934 and 1936, even now suggests the impact which they had at the time. Treece called the publication of *18 Poems* "a wordy

Geoffrey Grigson

revolution" against the *fin-de-siècle* period of disillusionment and disintegration in contemporary literary circles, with all political statements seeming suspect on the Right and the Left. It also assaulted the chaos and melancholy in poetic circles. How different were these poems by a nineteen-year-old from "Mr Eliot's *Waste Land* depression,

W. H. Davies's leisurely perusal of sheep and cows, Mr (Herbert) Reed's Great War reminiscences and Auden's telegraphese."

John Wain, in an acute recent article on Dylan called 'Druid of Her Broken Body', supports Treece in his view of his times. Wain corroborates that Dylan grew up in a bad literary period, in some ways worse than modern days. In the 1930s, there was a general assumption that the regions were dead and London was the source of all thought and intellect. Roots had to be chopped off, heritage denied, accents clipped to the standard speech of the metropolis. Dylan did not conform to the conventions of his time, neither to the social-conscience verses of Auden and his followers, nor to the wilful obscurities of the imported Breton school. As Wain says, logically applied Surrealism is as sure a recipe for mediocrity as logically applied Social Realism. Dylan looked resolutely into his inner adolescent world of symbol and myth, of sex and God and death. As he wrote to Treece at the time, enclosing his first draft of 'How Shall My Animal': "I hold a beast, an angel and a madman in me, and my enquiry is as to their working, and my problem is their subjugation and victory, downthrow and upheaval, and my effort is their self-expression."

Treece found *18 Poems* far superior to Dylan's next book of *Twenty-five Poems*. There is some merit in his judgement. The first volume represented the reworking of many of the best poems from the four Swansea *Notebooks*, while in the second volume, at least sixteen of the poems can be traced back to the same *Notebooks*. These versions were thus Dylan's second selection from the extraordinary outpourings of his adolescence. They often represent, perhaps as sops to Richard Church, the more simple poems of Dylan's youth, written before the *18 Poems*. When Treece attacked Dylan for apparently printing two styles of poetry in his second volume, and when he called the result "a poetic scrapbook", Dylan admitted to the charge. He had reworked "the straight poems" of his earliest period of the *Notebooks* and had leap-frogged them over the back of the volume of 1934 to appear for the first time in 1936. "Both books contain poems written over about eight years," Dylan wrote; "there is still no definite sequence."

Yet the simplicity of some of these poems and the championship of Edith Sitwell, who roundly declared that no other young poet showed so great an achievement, led to an unusual success for the second volume. Four editions were printed of *Twenty-five Poems* and three thousand copies were sold. Although other critics carped at Dylan, they could not detract from his unexpected success. Geoffrey Grigson might later declare that this minor celebrity in London was due to a confidence trick played by the poet on the public, but Treece and Wain and Fitzgibbon would all disagree. Dylan's limited success with his contemporaries was due to his unique gift for dealing with fundamentals in the lives of most people, with birth and death, with God and the Devil, with love and decay. Despite the obscurity of many of his poems of this period, a quality rooted in human nature always structures each poem, as the bones do the body.

The 'straight' poems of the second volume have become some of the most famous of Dylan's work. Perhaps, as Treece says, the first *18 Poems* have a "foetal unity" and are preoccupied with sex, at its most intense in 'I See The Boys Of Summer In Their Ruin' and 'The Force That Through The Green Fuse Drives The Flower'. Yet none of them has the urgent cadences, the sense of bardic incantation mixed with biblical memories, that lie in Dylan's modern psalm against dying, 'And Death Shall Have No Dominion'. If the ten sonnet-like sequences of 'Altarwise By Owl-light' are more wilfully obscure than anything in the first volume, yet the final versions of Dylan's earlier "straight poems" made him at last seem a true people's poet in 1936. 'This Bread I Break' is worthy to rank beside Dylan's denial of death in his *Twenty-five Poems*; these are the two great songs of the new bard of Wales at last reaching his true wide audience and flock.

> And death shall have no dominion.
> No more may gulls cry at their ears
> Or waves break loud on the seashores;
> Where blew a flower may a flower no more
> Lift its head to the blows of the rain;
> Though they be mad and dead as nails,
> Heads of the characters hammer through daisies;
> Break in the sun till the sun breaks down,
> And death shall have no dominion.

Peace Before War

I think a squirrel stumbling at least of equal importance as Hitler's invasions, murder in Spain, the Garbo-Stokowski romance, royalty, Horlicks, lynchlaw, pit disaster, Joe Louis, wicked capitalists, saintly communists, democracy, the Ashes, the Church of England, birth control, Yeats' voice, the machines of the world I tick and revolve in, pub-baby-weather-government-football-youthandage-speed-lipstick, all small tyrannies, means tests, the fascist anger, the daily, momentary lightnings, eruptions, farts, dampsquibs, barrel-organs, tinwhistles, howitzers, tiny death-rattles, volcanic whimpers of the world I eat, drink, love, work, hate and delight in – but I am aware of these things as well.

from a letter to Henry Treece by Dylan Thomas, 6th or 7th July, 1938

Opposite: *Portrait of Caitlin Macnamara by Augustus John.*

Peace Before War

Dylan met Caitlin Macnamara at a pub called the Wheatsheaf in Charlotte Street. It was April, 1936. They began an immediate affair, using the Eiffel Tower Hotel. As Fitzgibbon writes, Augustus John had introduced the young couple, but he did not know that their hotel bill was charged to him. Caitlin had, after all, grown up as his neighbour and had fallen very much under his spell and into his ageing arms. He did not know immediately of her new love, even if most of Fitzrovia did. Dylan was her own age, and his lethargic and intense character fitted marvellously with her own alternating rhythm of laziness and violent energy. She had trained as a free-style dancer in the mode of Isadora Duncan, and her flight from her parents' broken marriage and the decaying charms of the family mansion in Ireland had taken her to the passions and liberties of the John household, Paris and Soho. Now she returned to Augustus John, while Dylan went through his Surrealist fever and fell sick of it and decided that he loved Caitlin, after all.

The next meeting between the two of them led to a confrontation with Augustus John, who glossed over the affair in his autobiography. The three of them had met again at the Georgian house of the writer Richard Hughes, which was called the Castle because it adjoined the ruins of the old fortifications at Laugharne. They set off to visit the National Eisteddfod, which was being held in Fishguard that year near the circle of ancient Druid stones overlooking the old harbour. Caitlin and Dylan's public attraction for each other led finally to a drunken fight in a car-park between Dylan and Augustus John, in which the old painter knocked the young poet down and drove off with Caitlin into the night.

Dylan, however, kept on writing to Caitlin the love-letters of his joy and intentions. "I don't want you for a day," he wrote . . . "a day is the length of a gnat's life: I want you for the lifetime of a big, mad animal,

Opposite: *Augustus John*

95

like an elephant." His language then became that of one of the first of the flower children. "We'll always be young and unwise together. There is, I suppose, in the eyes of the They, a sort of sweet madness about you and me, a sort of mad bewilderment and astonishment oblivious to the Nasties and the Meanies; you're the only person, of course, you're the only person from here to Aldebaran and back, with whom I'm free entirely; and I think it's because you're as innocent as me." Naturally, they knew the lust and the dirty jokes and the dirty people, and they could count their change and cross the road, but their innocence was truly deep, so that they knew nothing much of the ways of the world, and did not care about that ignorance.

Such complete understanding led to their meeting in the Cornish summer of the following year. Both were penniless and free and in love. The only surprising fact was their sudden marriage on the 12th of July, in the Penzance registry office, "with no money, no prospect of money, no attendant friends or relatives, and in complete happiness." The reasons for the marriage seem to have been contradictory – a mutual latching onto a passion to last a lifetime; Dylan's fear of losing his girl again to Augustus John or another; his residue of Welsh puritanism and respectability that made him want to show his wife proudly to his family at his home; and finally the absurd belief at the heart of all first marriages for love, that the ceremony would magically end all problems instead of beginning them.

After such a glad beginning, the young lovers were lodgers at the mercy of family and friends. A visit to the new Thomas home at Swansea ended in the disapproval of Dylan's mother at Caitlin's gypsy dresses, so she and Dylan moved to her mother's house near Augustus John in Hampshire. There Dylan wrote to Watkins, "Caitlin & I ride into the New Forest every day, into Bluebell Wood or onto Cuckoo Hill . . . We are quiet and small and cigarette-stained and very young." As always, Dylan was living on nothing and looking to his friends for financial help. In a letter to Henry Treece, he wrote that he had suffered from living from his neighbours' hand to his mouth. "I have achieved poverty with distinction, but never poverty with dignity; the best I can manage is dignity with poverty." If he was going to go on writing any longer, he would have to give up living, and live in a vacuum.

Dylan's alternatives seemed limited to him. They were either the slow debts of the country or the quick debts of the city. Even in London,

Opposite: *Portrait of Richard Hughes in 1936 by Augustus John.*

he could still be living in penury and in doubt. "In London, because money lives and breeds there; in penury, because it doesn't; and in doubt as to whether I should continue as an outlaw or take my fate for a walk in the straight and bowler-treed paths." Of course, Dylan could never have measured out his days by commuter trains. He was no T. S. Eliot or Wallace Stevens, to fit his verses to his regular hours. He even laughed at his own bombast in thinking he could be a daily worker for bread or wages. "The conceit of outlaws is a wonderful thing", his letter continued. "They think they can join the ranks of regularly-conducted society whenever they like." He certainly could not.

As Caitlin later testified, Dylan never suffered from the usual doubts about his craft or the form of it. "From the minute he saw daylight: he had no choice but to write." All that seriously bothered him was the arrangement of patterns of words, "and which particular word, out of his glorious riches of words, was the most apt. That, and a continuous headache of debts." Between money and muse, poverty and craft, Dylan's marriage skimped and bloomed. Some money did somehow trickle in, from a poem here, a story there, from an occasional review, and even from the United States, where James Laughlin of New Directions was persuaded to buy up the rights on Dylan's next five books for a reasonable sum in dollars, to be paid weekly in a form of allowance. It was enough to help him move on to Laugharne, where Richard Hughes found Caitlin and him a fisherman's cottage for themselves.

So began Dylan's long association with Laugharne, which he had first seen in the black mood before his original sinful Gower affair in 1934. Then he had noticed its curious Englishness in manners and accent, although it was surrounded by hundreds of miles of Welsh countryside; it had seemed to him populated by a race of thick-lipped fools sweating their lives away cockling on the deadly sands. It was a church town rather than a chapel town with a polyglot population of Welsh descent, mixed with Dutch and English and Spanish blood. It was occupied rather than lived in, beleaguered as well as beguiling, with its chief function waiting for something to happen and living on the dole. As Dylan remembered later, it was an island of a town, where some people started to retire before they started to work, and others seemed "like Welsh opium-eaters, half asleep in a heavy bewildered daze."

With Caitlin pregnant, Laugharne was a haven for Dylan in the summer of 1938. The only worry, as always, was the bills. Although his

Opposite: *Dylan and Caitlin at Sea View, Laugharne.*

Laugharne Castle, and fishingboats on the "deadly sands".

publishers gave them a little regular money and his friends like Lawrence Durrell contributed the occasional pound, "crisper than celery and sweeter than sugar", he failed to get a grant from the Royal Literary Fund. Debt drove him back to Caitlin's mother's house for her to have the baby there; but pride brought him back to Laugharne again in the spring of 1939 and in the last seasons before the war.

Although Laugharne was cheap and comforting for Dylan, London could provide the only solution for his poverty. Yet in this country bliss of his, the skin-stripping capital had become hateful. As he wrote to Watkins after three dark days in London, it was an insane city of the restless dead. "Every pavement drills through your soles to your scalp, and out pops a lamp-post covered with hair. I'm not going to London again for years; its intelligentsia is so hurried in the head that nothing stays there; its glamour smells of goat; there's no difference between good & bad." Even if Laugharne was bitter and cruel because of small debts, yet he and Caitlin were happy there. If only it were not for money, and tiny sums of money at that. "The garret's repugnant," as Dylan complained to Treece. "I can't keep a steady hand and wag a wild tongue if worry like a bumbailiff sits silently nagging by my side. Poverty makes me lazy and crafty. I'm not a fineweather poet, or a lyrical tramp, or a bright little bowl waiting for the first fine flush, or a man who cuts his face with a grand phrase while shaving; I like regular meals and drink and a table and a ruler – and three pens."

So Dylan remained at heart roomed and domesticated. He wrote best when living within his comforts and spoiling by his women. In those early days of marriage, as Caitlin wrote, "Dylan may have been a skinny, springy lambkin, but I was more like its buxom mother then." She managed the little house and the baby on almost no money. She provided Dylan with his interminable stews, which he liked in his stomach before the solace of the pub, where she also went with him throughout the country years.

Rural living did not mellow Dylan's arrogance about his fellow writers. He was not one of those authors who find that a little fame of their own makes them able to forgive the abilities of their contemporaries. Dylan's book-reviews in the pre-war years show a continuing disrespect for the great names of the past and present. Emily Dickinson's poetry, arguably as good as William Blake's, is dismissed by Dylan as a curiosity, "the curiosity of a narrow abstract vision interpreted in legal, com-

Opposite: *Sea View, Laugharne.*

mercial, financial, and mathematical phraseology, furnished with the objective commonplaces of a life lived between the sewing basket and the bird bath, the Bible and the account book." Samuel Beckett's extraordinary novel *Murphy* seems the product of an Irish comic journalist forced to write in an advanced Paris-American quarterly, or of an old-fashioned music-hall character-comedian trying to alter his act for a pornographer's club, "and always it is Freudian blarney: Sodom and Begorrah." William Carlos Williams's reputation is built up like a pack of visiting cards, while his *Life Along the Passaic River* is ruined by "the affected *and* insipid convention of trying to write like an enemy of writing." H. G. Wells is a specimen of "the boy who never grows up; a sort of Peter Bedpan." John Dos Passos's masterpiece, *U.S.A.*, is the uncondensed material for the Great American Novel, "that ton of a dry dream which has ruined beyond repair such a number of ambitious men," while the structure of the novel opens, like a bolstered bosom, to let us all in. Even Kafka's *Amerika* has a beginning and a tail, no middle and no sting. Only Flann O'Brien gets a pat on the head for his *At Swim-Two-Birds* and for being at the forefront of modern Irish literature among several others, whose names Dylan pretends not to remember; while the incomparable Djuna Barnes is eulogised for her *Nightwood* – Dylan could hardly stay out of that choir of contemporary praise.

On the eve of war in 1939, Dylan published his third book, *The Map of Love*. He included some of his mythological and Surrealist stories, which he had hoped to publish under the title of *The Burning Baby*. It also included the last of the overworked poems taken from his four Swansea *Notebooks*. Of the sixteen poems in *The Map of Love*, eleven seem to date from his adolescence, of which eight were merely pruned rather than rewritten. While 'How Shall My Animal' is completely worded anew except for the first line, Dylan only actually wrote five new poems in the two and a half pre-war years of the beginning of his relationship with Caitlin.

These new poems show Dylan consciously trying to be simpler and stronger. In 'After the Funeral' at last he admits to the reality and melancholy of his loved aunt's end.

> . . . her death was a still drop;
> She would not have me sinking in the holy
> Flood of her heart's fame; she would lie dumb and deep
> And need no druid of her broken body.

But I, Ann's bard on a raised hearth, call all
The seas to service that her wood-tongued virtue
Babble like a bellbuoy over the hymning heads, . .

Dylan no longer showed the bombastic and self-conscious pretence of uncaring for family death, chronicled in his youthful letter to Trevor Hughes of January, 1933, when he had tried to ignore his aunt dying of cancer of the womb. Then he had boasted of "the pleasant death-reek at my negroid nostrils", and had declared that he had not the faintest interest in her or her womb, and would only miss her bi-annual postal orders. Now that he had grown into love of Caitlin, Dylan had also grown into a respect for death, including his own.

That respect also shows in his powerful new poem, beginning:

Twenty-four years remind the tears of my eyes.
(Bury the dead for fear that they walk to the grave in labour) . . .

Dylan remained obsessed by the fact that his end was natural and inevitable, but at the moment he was more occupied with his sensual strut. Yet even the delights and sloths and respectabilities and com-

Dylan and his mother visit the graveyard where Aunt Annie Jones is buried.

mitments of marriage had their price. They kept him away from his true calling. The best poem in *The Map of Love* is Dylan's life-long cry from the heart at his failure to write more poems.

> On no work of words now for three lean months in the bloody
> Belly of the rich year and the big purse of my body
> I bitterly take to task my poverty and craft.
>
> To take to give is all, return what is hungrily given
> Puffing the pounds of manna up through the dew to heaven,
> The lovely gift of the gab bangs back on a blind shaft . . .

When the timeless time-wasting days of first marriage began to be counted in babies and hours, the war had begun. The lovely gift of the gab was not to work much on poems for a decade, only at the warm running pieces of memory that begin in the stories of *Portrait of the Artist as a Young Dog* and end in the nostalgic B.B.C. pieces of his last years. Dylan's friend Vernon Watkins noticed how suddenly Dylan began to write about people as they actually were and behaved. As for the stories of Dylan's youth, "very Welsh they were, more true to Swansea than Swansea itself." This collection of autobiographical pieces gives the exaggerated essence of the place, a reality that can be recalled rather than seen. The nostalgia was mixed with both comedy and irony, and if the title of the book owed something to James Joyce's *A Portrait of the Artist as a Young Man*, Dylan always denied that he had read a word of the Irishman's memoirs before writing his own book – but then, as Caitlin always said, Dylan had a congenital passion for lies.

These Swansea tales are Dylan's most coherent work in prose. Although each story is self-contained, taking Dylan from Fern Hill in his boyhood to the pubs of Swansea beach of his young manhood, yet they serve as the ten windows of an upbringing that was as solid and semi-detached as an Uplands villa. Dylan's wicked observing of Welsh observances, both social and Sunday ones, make the stories a comic delight. In the first story, 'The Peaches', where plump Mrs Williams with the big car visits the poor farm-wife Annie, she refuses the hoarded tinned delicacy of the title with the squashing and self-revealing remark, "No, no, Mrs Jones, thanks the same . . . I don't mind pears or chunks, but I can't bear peaches." Such small-town snobbery is a gift to Dylan's sense of mimicry and skill at word-play.

Opposite: *Dylan Thomas in Wales in about 1938.*

The other themes of the poet sound through the stories. The boy Dylan staying at his grandfather's cottage dreams of "heavenly choirs in the sticks, dressed in bard's robes and brass-buttoned waistcoats," while his grandfather goes off to be buried in his ancestral ground at Llangadock before his time, "like a prophet who has no doubt." Sex shows its fumblings and misdirections and impossibilities in the triangle of Patricia and Edith and Arnold, in the bullied calf-love of Extraordinary Little Cough, in the unmeant squalor of 'Just Like Little Dogs' where the brothers exchange girls on the night sand, and finally in the climb through the labyrinth of the guest-house stairs to the lost Lou of 'One Warm Saturday' in which Dylan mourns the unapproachable pub women of his adolescence who later smothered him in his London years. Schoolboy humour and cheeky jokes, pub chatter and mock-tough talk, make real the adjectival paragraphs of overblown description of self and town, with Dylan remembering when "the eccentric ordinary people came bursting and crawling, with noise and colours, out of their houses, out of the graceless buildings, the factories and avenues, the shining shops and blaspheming chapels, the terminuses and the meeting-halls, the falling alleys and brick lanes, from the arches and shelters and holes behind the hoardings, out of the common, wild intelligence of the town."

When the British government declared war on Germany in 1939, Dylan's first reaction was both cowardly and unpatriotic, although he did not see the choice in those terms. He wrote to his new patron and friend, John Davenport, that he was desperate to get a job, because all the unemployed were going to be conscripted. "My one-&-only body I will not give." He did have his name put down for work at the Ministry of Information, on the "crook list" with "all the half-poets, the boiled newspapermen, submen from the islands of crabs, dismissed advertisers, old mercuries, mass-snoopers"; but nothing came of it. The outbreak of war seemed to Dylan to be a deliberate attack on himself and his powers of poetry. He complained of the beginning of "Dylan-shooting" in a copy of *The Map of Love* dedicated to Pamela Hansford Johnson. He had not the means to flee to neutral America like W. H. Auden and Christopher Isherwood. So he chose the path of trying to become a conscientious objector, not from religious scruples, but simply from a distaste for the disruption of his own life. As he wrote to Bert Trick, "I

Opposite: *Christopher Isherwood* (left) *and W. H. Auden* (right) *leave London for China in 1938.*

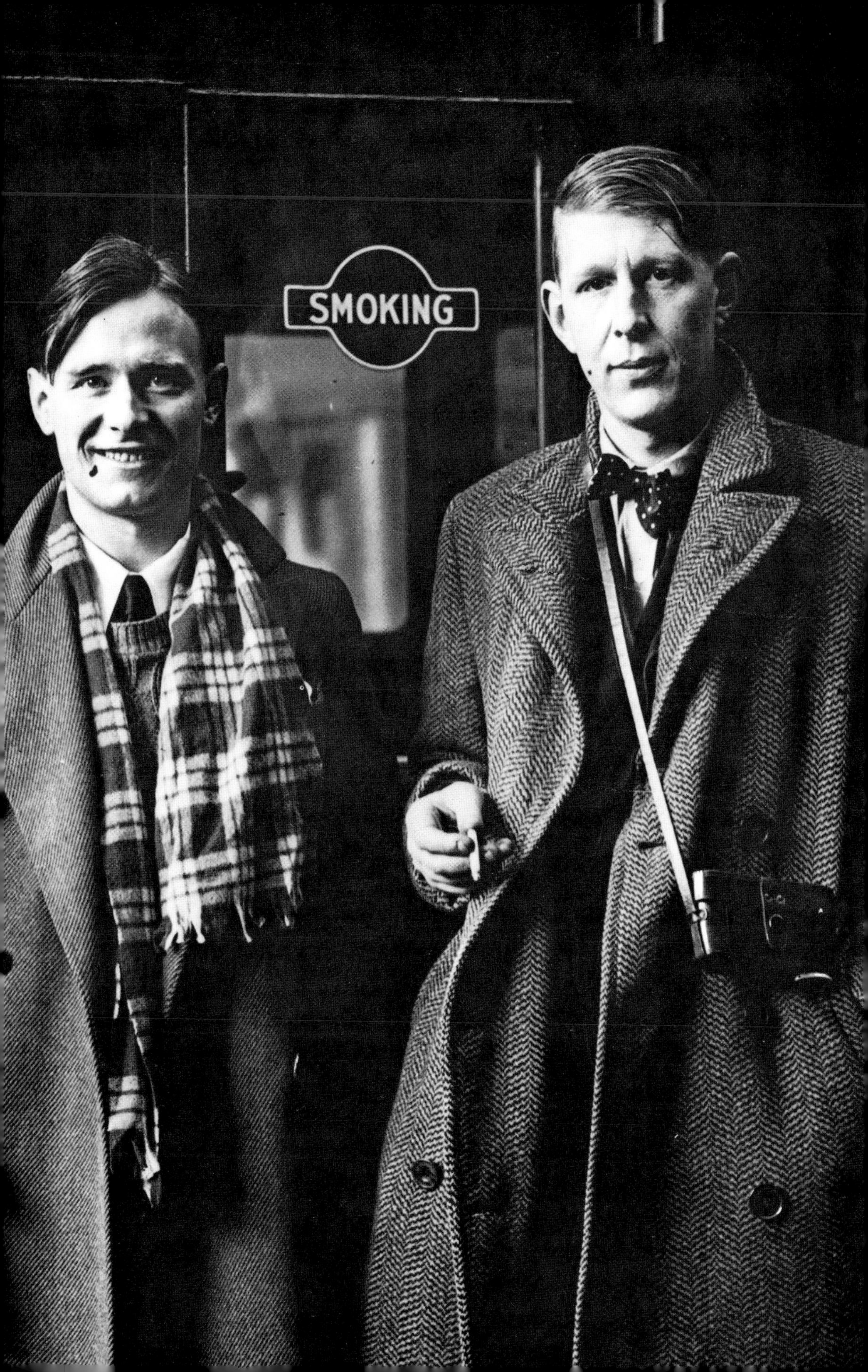
SMOKING

can't raise up any feeling about this war at all. And the demon Hitlerism can go up to its own bottom. I refuse to help it with a bayonet."

Friendship and physical incapacity luckily solved the problems of Dylan's selfish pacifism. When he tried to encourage his literary acquaintances to contribute to a symposium in support of his objector's position before he was called to a tribunal, he usually received a cold shoulder or a hot reply to his effort to form "a common or rarefied front or backside". When his time for the tribunal came, however, Dylan found he could not stomach a plea of religion as an excuse not to fight, so he did not plead at all. Instead, the army medical examiners in their mercy diagnosed him as an acute asthmatic and he was graded at the bottom level of those fit to soldier. If war was not Dylan's concern, those who ran the war were equally unconcerned about him.

So Dylan's pacifist bluster ended in a whimper. More real was the problem of debt. He had to raise £70 to stop himself and his family from being turned out of their cottage in Laugharne, with all their possessions seized. Stephen Spender organised an appeal which was sent to leading literary figures. The money soon was found, with a small surplus. It was a rare tribute to Dylan from a group of writers, whom Dylan rarely praised and was to parody to literary death in his unpublished and libellous novel, *The Death of the King's Canary*.

The work was written during 1940 on a drunken stay in the Cotswolds with John Davenport at The Malting House, where Davenport used to entertain writers and musicians seeking escape from the war. Alternate chapters and even pages were written by the two collaborators, but the manuscript is unfunny without being ironic, harsh without being penetrating. The plot deals with the choice of a successor to a dead Poet Laureate, and it lampoons the bad behaviour of most of the living authors whom Dylan envied. The one affectionate portrait is naturally reserved for Dylan's fantasy self, who is a young and handsome Welsh poet called Owen Tudor with a dark and subtle look, as thin as Dylan had now become stout and beer-bellied. One line only from Owen Tudor prophesies the self-mocking comedy of Dylan's later style: "When I am a rich man with my own bicycle and can have beer for breakfast, I shall give up writing poetry altogether and just be absolutely disgusting."

It was the war, however, and lack of riches that stopped Dylan from writing poetry and set him on the absolutely disgusting search for a job.

Opposite: *Stephen Spender*

Eight Years Older
and Deeper in Debt

On top of bills & writs, all howlingly pressing, I must get out of here & find somewhere else to live at once. And that will take money, which I haven't got. All I earn I spend & give to past debts. I'm in a mess all right. But I know I could write a good new script. And I wish Redgrave & Rank would pay me to do it.

from a letter by Dylan Thomas to Graham Greene, 11th January, 1947

Opposite: *Portrait of Dylan Thomas in 1940 by Rupert Shephard.*

Eight Years Older
and Deeper in Debt

As war broke out, Dylan began looking both for a way not to die and a way to keep alive. The film industry seemed a possibility. Dylan wrote to John Davenport from Laugharne: "Does the film-world want an intelligent young man of literary ability, self-conscious, punch-drunk, who must (for his own sake) keep out of the bloody war, who's willing to do any work – provided of course that it pays enough for living? I'm not expecting plums from the war . . ." John Davenport could not help Dylan; but in 1940, Dylan met Ivan Moffatt, the son of the actress Iris Tree. Moffatt was working for Strand Films, a company run by Donald Taylor and deputed by the Ministry of Information to make many of its short films, which were designed to boost morale on the home front. Taylor recognised the need for good writers of prose as well as efficient script-writers. In the film-struck Dylan, he found a marvellous journey-man with words and a pupil at film technique.

As a boy, Dylan had always loved the cinema. In *Return Journey*, he wrote of "the flea-pit picture-house where he whooped for the scalping Indians with Jack Basset and banged for the rustlers' guns." With his café friends in Swansea, films were always part of the gossip and gibble-gabble, as they talked about "Augustus John, Emil Jannings, Carnera, Dracula, Amy Johnson, trial marriage, pocket-money, the Welsh sea, the London stars, King Kong . . ." In his spoof play written for Pamela Hansford Johnson, *Spajma and Salnady: Or Who Shot the Emu?*, Dylan explained his nineteen-year-old cinema taste as particularly influenced by German expressionism, including: *The Cabinet of Dr. Caligari, Atalanta, The Student of Prague, The Edge of the World, Vaudeville, Waxworks, The Street, M,* and *The Blue Angel*, with *Sous les Toits de Paris, Potemkin, The Gold Rush, The Three Little Pigs,* and the Marx Brothers' comedies thrown in for good measure. Otherwise, he claimed rarely to go to the pictures, as the vast majority of films was notoriously bad. As for Norma Shearer, Lionel Barrymore, Clark

Gable, George Raft, Joan Crawford, Uncle Tom Navarro and all, he preferred "abstruse poetry, symbolical fiction, discordant music, and beer."

In fact, Dylan was far more serious about the cinema than he pretended. He had revealed his interest in the subject while still at school. There he had contributed to the *Swansea Grammar School Magazine* an article on the development of the modern cinema from D. W. Griffith to the coming of sound. If his judgements were adolescent, his sense of the future of the medium was evident. Sound was all-important, both to him and the film industry. The article ended: "Even film-pioneers must start at the beginning of sound-film production, and learn what there is to be learnt."

Dylan started as a film-pioneer in sound film production at £8 a week for Strand Films, later increased to £10 a week. Since he was alarmed by the bombing in London, he was allowed to write wherever he wished. On his visits to London, most of the script conferences were held in pubs or in the Café Royal at the producer's expense, so Dylan felt a new ease as well as a new career opening in front of him. His old existence as a poet seemed expendable. As he was to write in one of his screenplays, "when one burns one's boats, what a very nice fire it makes." His arson was at Bertram Rota, the rare-book seller, who bought Dylan's four *Notebooks* off him in 1941. Since Dylan had used these *Notebooks* as the quarries for more than half of his published poetry, it was an act of suttee.

Constantine Fitzgibbon suggests that Dylan's act was an imitation of Keats, long Dylan's mythical hero. Dylan had not died young of rotten lungs as Keats had. Now at the age of Keats's death, twenty-six years old, Dylan could kill poetry forever in himself, and, like the young Rimbaud, seek his future in the golden Abyssinia of Wardour Street. As his friend and co-screenwriter Maclaren Ross wrote of Dylan: "he was extremely interested in the film-medium," though he did not have "the true Documentary Mind."

At first, Dylan not only wrote documentary scripts, but provided the voice behind the sound-tracks. In Basil Wright's *This Is Colour*, he spoke with Valentine Dyall and others. He was the sole script-writer in *New Towns for Old*, which dealt pleasantly with the problems of commentary by throwing this plea for the reconstruction of industrial towns after the war into a dialogue between two voices – the later technique of the opening of *Under Milk Wood*. He co-operated with Ivan Moffatt on *Balloon Site 568*, a propaganda film encouraging recruits in the barrage

balloon service with its "floppy elephantine charges". He also worked on documentaries about the Council for the Encouragement of Music and Art, *The Conquest of a Germ* by penicillin, and on a deflation of Nazism called *These Are the Men*. In this, Dylan's ironic verse was super-imposed on a shortened version of Leni Riefenstahl's *Triumph of the Will*; Hitler and Goebbels and Goering and the Nuremberg Rally leaders are made to confess their errors, as if injected by a truth drug. The anonymous critic of the contemporary *Documentary News Letter* praised Dylan for verse which "frequently cuts like a knife into the pompously bestial affectations of this race of supermen."

Yet Dylan's apogee as a documentary script-writer was achieved, not in his pedestrian *Wales – Green Mountain, Black Mountain*, but in his more ambitious *Our Country*. In this loose and lingering look at war-time Britain that wanders through the Liverpool docks, blitzed London, the hopfields and airfields of Kent, the mines of South Wales and steel works of Sheffield, to end up in some strange West Indian lumber yards in Scotland and a bottle of rum in an Aberdeen trawler, Dylan's words do not impose themselves on the visuals. Through the medium of Jo Jago's camera and the narrator, a merchant seaman who wanders around wartime Britain, Dylan and the director John Eldridge produced a propaganda documentary which one critic in 1944 thought "the sole and successful experimental film of the war period." Its success went to Dylan's head and his two last documentaries were never released; *Is Your Earnie Really Necessary?* was suppressed by the Ministry as a lampoon after its first screening, while *Where Are They Now?* was never shown at all.

Dylan was always thought by Caitlin and his literary friends to be wasting his time and his genius as a script-writer. But he himself chose to be connected with films. He was not conscripted, he volunteered. If his asthma had not prevented his conscription into the army, he would have wasted out the war as a clerk in some camp. As it was, the writing of documentaries was his warwork and his wages. For the first time in his married life, he earned a regular salary in a job that did not prevent him from writing poetry, if he had wanted to do so. He did sometimes object to the conditions of the work with "dishonest men with hangovers", saying in one letter that he was writing from "a ringing, clinging office with repressed women all around punishing typewriters, and queers in striped suits talking about 'Cinema' and, just at this very moment, a

Opposite: *Dylan Thomas in 1947.*

man with a bloodhound's voice and his cheeks, I'm sure, full of Mars Bars, rehearsing out loud a radio talk on 'India and the Documentary Movement.'" Yet Dylan, in fact, was a talented script-writer who improved from documentary to documentary, who was contributing both to the war effort and to his family's upkeep, and finally, who was escaping from that dreaded solitude that is the necessary confinement of poets.

For film-making is a sociable trade. It solves the problem of the writer, that desperate seclusion with blank pages, which, even if covered with words, have no audience until they lie dead on the printed page years after the event. The social animal in Dylan as well as the actor in him adored the quick translation of words to screen through the medium of the actual life of people that the British wartime school of documentary tried to capture. If Dylan was only a craftsman at films and not an artist, yet even its despised techniques helped him as a poet. Commentaries, by their nature, have to be clear. They have to be unobtrusive behind the visuals. Dylan's early verse style tended to obscurity and exaggerated metaphor. His stint as a documentary writer for Strand Films taught him economy, precision and simplicity of expression. His major post-war poems such as 'Fern Hill', 'In Country Sleep', 'Lament', 'Do Not Go Gentle Into That Good Night', and 'Prologue', seem to have benefited from that workaday wartime need to communicate with the people of Britain in as clear a voice as possible.

Dylan's efforts to write feature films after the war are harder to defend. The British Broadcasting Corporation began to employ him fairly regularly; but like many other writers, he looked to a sold screenplay to solve his financial problems. At first, Donald Taylor kept him on his retainer, putting him to work on the screenplay of Maurice O'Sullivan's charming book about growing up in the Blaskets, wild islands off the coast of Ireland. The half-finished screenplay owes much to Dylan's perfect understanding of O'Sullivan's loved country boyhood; but as a film, it is more Flaherty and documentary than feature film.

Soon, Taylor switched Dylan onto a script called *Suffer Little Children*, after trying him on a script on Labour, although Dylan protested he was not "politically very acute" and would have to "rely, as always, upon emotionalism." *Suffer Little Children* was also never made, although some of the dialogue sequences ended in a Diana Dors

Opposite: *Dylan plays shove-halfpenny in a Chelsea pub in 1946.*

vehicle called *Good Time Girl*. Dylan kept complaining to Taylor that he could not live in New Quay in 1945 on his retainer, now cut again to £8 a week; but he went on trying to complete a salable feature script, after abortive attempts to deal with the lives of Robert Burns and Crippen.

Another subject suggested by Donald Taylor to Dylan during this period was the bodysnatching of Burke and Hare, and Dylan finished the script under the title of *The Doctor and the Devils*. Taylor was interested in the character of the historical Dr Knox, who needed the corpses supplied by the two Edinburgh resurrectionists for his studies in anatomy in the early nineteenth century. Although inspired by James Bridie's play *The Anatomist*, Taylor and Thomas seem to have ignored the successful version of the subject made with Boris Karloff, *The Bodysnatchers*. The new script, however, is full of touches of the best of Dylan's conjuring prose. The opening sequences have such passages as:

> The straw-strewn cobbles of the Market are crowded with stalls. Stalls that sell rags and bones, kept by rags and bones. Stalls that sell odds and ends of every odd kind, odd boots, bits of old meat, fish heads, trinkets, hats with feathers, broadsheets, hammers. Stalls with shawls. Stalls like ash bins. . . . There are many, many children, some very old.

Dylan used to call such passages his "descriptive-visual" writing, and wonderfully evocative they are. To his friend Maclaren Ross, he declared his intention of writing a "complete scenario ready for shooting which would give the ordinary reader an absolute visual impression of the film in words and could be published as a new form of literature."

Eisenstein had once proved that a paragraph of Dickens could be broken down, each phrase a separate shot, and it could become a perfect sequence, so immediate and apt were the succession of words and the placing of the commas. Dylan certainly had the same intentions and qualities in his powerful and just descriptions of action. It was his dialogue that was, frankly, too literary for the medium, which is a mass art. One speech Dylan gives to Doctor Rock (Knox) in *The Doctor and the Devils* shows this elegant failure.

> ROCK'S VOICE ". . . When I said, cool as ice, one morning – cool as fire! – 'Elizabeth and I are married.' Oh, the shame and horror on the faces of all the puritanical hyenas, prudery ready to pounce and bite, snobbery braying in all the drawing-rooms and breeding-boxes, false pride and prejudice coming

out of their holes, hissing and spitting because a man married for love and not for property or position nor for any of the dirty devices of the world . . ."

With description an inspiration for any director and dialogue better off on the stage, Dylan allied a competent film construction technique which drove the story forward on Taylor's suggestion. The style may seem old-fashioned now, in the manner of those well-made British historical dramas, long on education and short on action. But in its time, it even seemed excessive. For fear of censorship, it largely avoided violence, despite the fact that sixteen murders were committed by Broom (Burke) and Fallon (Hare) to provide fresh corpses for the anatomists. The smothering of the victims is suggested, not seen. The outrage is in the trenchant cynicism of the offensive Doctor Rock. "When *I* take up assassination," Rock is made to say, "I shall start with the surgeons in this city and work *up* to the gutter." Or explaining the fresh corpses brought by his bodysnatchers, Rock declares, "They are corpse-diviners. Or, as some have green fingers for gardening, so they have black fingers for death. Do you expect the dead to walk here, Tom? They need assistance."

Dylan had been obsessed in his pre-war days with shocking prose, with blood and guts all over the Surrealist paragraphs of *The Map of Love*. So it is curious to find him so restrained in his best screenplay, although it deals with bodysnatchers. Perhaps, as in the good films of Dylan's contemporary, Val Lewton, the horror in *The Doctor and the Devils* was best suggested, not depicted. Yet Lewton dealt with psychological terror, not a succession of murders. And Dylan's talent for prose was, at the last resort, too great for his subject.

Although Dylan begged Graham Greene early in 1947 to help him in getting the screenplay made, it never has been. Greene said that he liked the script and Dylan thanked him for it – "if anyone could *like* such a nasty thing." He begged Greene to secure him more film work from Rank to pay his bills, writing: "I want, naturally, to write a hundred-times-better script, and I'm sure I can. I can write other than horrible stories, and I want to."

In fact, Dylan did get more film work in 1948. For British National Pictures, he polished the dialogue of two films directed by Dan Birt, *Three Weird Sisters* and *No Room at the Inn*. Then he progressed to writing for Gainsborough Pictures, for whom he worked on three films;

all these scripts have been published. The first of them was called *The Beach at Falesá* and was taken from a story by Robert Louis Stevenson. There is little merit in this script by Dylan, nor in his extended treatment of the Welsh revolt of 1843 against toll-gates, called *Rebecca's Daughters*. This second screenplay is, actually, a ten-times-worse piece of work than *The Doctor and the Devils*, with cardboard characterisations of English gentry and Welsh rebels, and terrible dialogue such as "Mayhap you stopped at the Black Lion."

The only other available piece of Dylan's screenwriting is the first section of an original film operetta called *Me and my Bike*, which Dylan wrote for Sydney Box. Dylan wrote to a friend about his enthusiasm for the project, because Box had given him "carte blanche as to freedom of fancy, non-naturalistic dialogue, song, music, etc . . ." But Dylan performed an incomplete and shoddy job on this final script of his, for he was already too busy on "judging, my God, Poetry Festivals, and Third-Programming." If there is a saving grace in *Me and My Bike*, it is in Thomas's idea for the film, covering the whole span of the life of a man, who "rides penny-farthings, tandems, tricycles, racing bikes – and when he dies at the end, he rides on his bike up a sunbeam straight to heaven, where he's greeted by a heavenly chorus of bicycle bells." But as for the execution of the lyrics, it is hurried and facile, with lines reading like inferior Ogden Nash, such as:

> . . . Man's Best Friend is the horse
> Everybody agrees
> But when I say gee it whoas up
> And when I say whoa it gees up, knees up;
> When I say whoa it gees.

So ended Dylan's screen-writing period which lasted for eight years. It brought him a regular salary, some gain in clarity, and some waste of his poetic years. His next regular patron, which was to encourage his best work and pay him badly for it, was the British Broadcasting Corporation. Between his wars with its contracts department and His Majesty's Inspector of Taxes, who had discovered by 1948 that Dylan had never filled in a tax form, the poet spent the last five years of his life in a straightjacket of debt, with half his earnings from more than forty broadcasts deducted at source by the tax collector, as well as most of the money from Gainsborough Pictures. The effort to solve his financial worries by film-writing had left Dylan only deeper in debt. He had already presaged his fate in his early poem, 'Our Eunuch Dreams':

Dylan at the BBC in 1946, with Patric Dickinson, head of poetry programmes.

. . . In this our age the gunman and his moll,
   Two one-dimensioned ghosts, love on a reel,
   Strange to our solid eye,
   And speak their midnight nothings as they swell;
   When cameras shut they hurry to their hole
   Down in the yard of day...

This is the world: the lying likeness of
   Our strips of stuff that tatter as we move
   Loving and being loth;
   The dream that kicks the buried from their sack
   And lets their trash be honoured as the quick.
   This is the world. Have faith.

View of New Quay.

The War at Home

*The home was to Dylan, more especially, a private sanctum,
where for once he was not compelled, by himself admittedly,
to put on an act, to be amusing, to perpetuate the myth of the
Enfant Terrible: one of the most damaging myths, and a curse
to grow out of. We lived almost separate lives, though physically
close, and passed each other with a detached phrase on strictly
practical matters; as though we were no more than familiar
landmarks, in the furniture of our minds. Excluding the times,
more frequent at night, when the house rattled, and banged, and
thudded, and groaned with our murder of each other.*

from *Leftover Life To Kill* CAITLIN THOMAS

The War at Home

At the birth of his first son Llewelyn, "a fat, round, bald, loud child, with a spread nose and blue saucer eyes", Dylan felt a surge of Welsh feeling and named the boy after a historical hero. As he wrote to Bert Trick of the baby, "he sounds militantly Welsh, and, though this is probably national pride seen through paternal imagination or vice-versa, he looks it too." The baby at first led to a closeness in the marriage with Caitlin, but soon the pressures of the war and of living from friends' room to parents' home, from hand to debt and month to mouth meant that Llewelyn stayed with Caitlin's mother, while the new baby, Aeronwy, stayed with Caitlin and Dylan in their single Chelsea room in London, their only secure base in the war years between a succession of makeshift homes in Swansea and Cardiganshire and even in Sir Alan Herbert's empty studio in Hammersmith. To say that the Thomases travelled light would be to exaggerate; they wandered with nothing at all. In 1942, Dylan summarised his possessions as not enough even to fill a mouse's home. "It is very good sometimes to have nothing," he wrote with bravado; "I want society, not me, to have places to sit in and beds to lie in; and who wants a hatstand of his very own?"

His wife did, and so did he. Their Chelsea studio was occupied by a large double-bed, a baby's bassinet, a gramophone and records; on the walls, reproductions of Henry Moore's drawings of people sleeping in air-raid shelters were put up alongside Dylan's own efforts at scratching pictures. In these cramped conditions, Dylan made himself comfortable enough, spending his days with the film men in Wardour Street and his evenings in the Chelsea pubs, sometimes insulting soldiers for the hell of it, and excusing his own lack of doing much for his country by pretending that he did not care much about what his country was doing.

His war poems, few as they are, contradicted his public attitude of cynicism and alienation. In particular, 'Ceremony After a Fire Raid' showed a profound grief at the shock of war and its outrageous murder of an innocent baby.

. . . Into the centuries of the child
  Myselves grieve now, and miracles cannot atone.

Yet the tragedy of dying never translated itself in Dylan into the catharsis of hating an enemy, a people, Germans. He would rather drink the war away, work on his short films, and pretend a detachment which concealed his inward preoccupations and obsessions that did not change.

  Even Caitlin at the time, although not in retrospect, was deceived by Dylan's deliberate waste of himself in London life, by his pose as the world-weary pub-crawler, disgusted with life. In an extraordinary memoir quoted by Fitzgibbon, a friend called Jack Lindsay told of

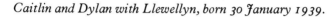

Caitlin and Dylan with Llewellyn, born 30 January 1939.

going to the Chelsea studio to find that Dylan had torn up all his poems the night before and had thrown them into the rubbish-bin. To Lindsay, it was Caitlin's job to rescue the poems from the rubbish when life got too much for the poet. But she refused, saying it was the last thing she would do. "Dylan's corrupt. Corrupt right through and through. It's not for me to save him from himself. If he can't do it himself, let him rot."

Naturally, Caitlin knew her man and naturally he had to salvage his poems himself. To throw them away had been an act of self-drama, not one of self-despair. Although the sale of the four Swansea *Notebooks* to Bertram Rota had ended Dylan's body-snatching of poetry from the corpse of his youth, he did not stop working on the new poems of his manhood, which were usually published in the one literary redoubt of the war years, Cyril Connolly's *Horizon* magazine. Connolly spoke of Dylan at that time, before he was mobbed to death in America like Orpheus and the Thracian women. "In the war years he could still look very fresh and attractive, although his cynical *persona* had descended on him. He really preferred to enclose all literary conversation in a kind of capsule of ridicule and parody. I used to buy his poems spot cash from his wallet as if they were packets of cocaine. . . ."

Dylan hardly wrote the few poems he finished in London, except when he was on his own. His most fertile period was at the end of the war, when he managed to find a bungalow for his family at New Quay, a tidy retirement seaside town in Wales that was to provide the geography for *Under Milk Wood*, even if much of the essence of the play came from memories of Laugharne. There at Majoda, an asbestos villa, Dylan once again proved what Caitlin always fought for and fought him for, that he could only write his best poems in the dull, contentious, close bosom of his family – and recover from it and them in the everyday evenings at the pub, where Caitlin had to join him to keep him near.

Pubbing, she was to discover, also became easy for her like most pernicious habits. She welcomed "the noisy, tapped and lamped cosiness . . . the burning upward rush to the head; then the lullabying coma of the alcohol." In the end the pub became for her almost what it was for Dylan, "a home: more homely than our own; from home." She could not remember one isolated evening that she had spent with Dylan at their house; there may never have been one. "To contemplate living without a pub to go back to; was homelessness indeed. A long,

Opposite: *Caitlin and Dylan in their Chelsea studio in 1944.*

Dylan and Caitlin drinking in Brown's Hotel, Laugharne.

homeless blank to fill up; like a sheet of blank paper with no inspiration. With no boozing pals in it, to fill it with homely life."

The particular pub in New Quay, which was their home from home and the refuge from the blank pages that might become poems or film-scripts, was the Black Lion. This pub was recorded by Dylan in one of his rhyming parodies of verse sent to his friend T. W. Earp. The poem was called 'New Quay' and held echoes of the Llareggub to come, from No-good Boyo to the prurient Jack Black and Evans the Death.

> . . . No-good is abroad. I unhardy can
> Hardly bear the din of No-good wracked dry on
> The pebbles. It is time for the Black Lion . . .
> I sit at the open window, observing
> The salty scene and my Playered gob curving
> Down to the wild, umbrella'd, and french lettered

Beach, hearing rise slimy from the Welsh lechered
Caves the cries of the parchs and their flocks. I
Hear their laughter sly as gonococci.
There stinks a snoop in black. I'm thinking it
Is Mr. Jones the Cake, that winking-bit,
That hymning Gooseberry, that Bethel-worm . . .
Sniff, here is sin! Now he must grapple, rise:
He snuggles deep among the chapel thighs,
And when the moist collection plate is passed
Puts in his penny, generous at last.

Although such poems were largely spoof and foolery, they did hold
the seed of Dylan's best comic writing to come; and at New Quay,
Dylan did also toil at some of the finer poems in his next volume, *Deaths
and Entrances*. If he had a literary conscience at the time, it was Vernon
Watkins. Although Watkins was serving in the Air Force and lost
Dylan's letters to him in the mid-war years, enough letters from Dylan
survive to show that the serious poet was begging to be let out of the
paunchy cynic of the bar-room. The surviving letters show Dylan at
his most warm-hearted and open, with all his adolescent defences
dropped to his friend, who even asked him to be best man at his wedding,
only for Dylan not to turn up, apologising for "reeking & rocking back
from a whirled London where nothing went right, all duties were left,
and my name spun rank in the whole smokey nose." But he sent to
Watkins from Wales copies of 'Poem In October', 'Holy Spring', 'A
Winter's Tale', 'The Conversation of Prayer', 'This Side Of The
Truth', and 'A Refusal To Mourn The Death, By Fire, Of A Child In
London'. Soon afterwards in 1945, Dylan wrote his two masterpieces,
'Fern Hill' and 'In My Craft Or Sullen Art'. The year of the end of
the war and Dylan's return to Wales brought about the flowering of
his genius as a poet.

A reading of the poems in *Deaths and Entrances*, which was printed
in 1946 and set the seal of critical approval on Dylan's reputation,
shows how Dylan's hackwork on film-scripts and reviews and occasional
prose pieces for broadcasting had wonderfully improved the clarity of
his poems. The balance and ease and sensuousness of 'Poem In October'
and 'Fern Hill' were the true labours of a man who had grown out of
the wilful obscurities of youth into the careful simplicities of age. It is
inconceivable that the young Dylan would have dared to be as direct
and romantic as the mature poet in his contemplation of his work.

In my craft or sullen art
Exercised in the still night
When only the moon rages
And the lovers lie abed
With all their griefs in their arms,
I labour by singing light
Not for ambition or bread
Or the strut and trade of charms

Left and above: *Dylan, Caitlin and their daughter Aeronwy at Laugharne in about 1945.*

> On the ivory stages
> But for the common wages
> Of their most secret heart . . .

If Dylan had written very few poems in the war years, yet his disgust at his experiences then seems to have allowed a pent love of country Wales to well out of the poems of that year of his return to a sea-town in Cardigan. To say that his film work or his later broadcasting was to prevent him from writing more or better poems would be untrue. Dylan himself never claimed such an easy way out of his responsibilities as a poet. Once a man, he did not think that living by writing other things than poems was a waste of himself. As he wrote to *Horizon* in 1946 in answer to questions on 'The Cost of Letters':

> Shadily living by one's literary wits is as good a way of making too little money as any other, so long as, all the time you are writing B.B.C. and film-scripts, reviews, etc., you aren't thinking, sincerely, that this work is depriving the

world of a great poem or a great story. Great, or at any rate very good, poems and stories do get written in spite of the fact that the writers of them spend much of their waking time doing entirely different things. And even a poet like Yeats, who was made by patronage financially safe so that he need not write and think nothing but poetry, *had*, voluntarily, to give himself a secondary job: that of philosopher, mystic, crank, quack.

It is arguable that Dylan needed to be deprived by the conditions of his life from writing poems in order to let them concentrate and clarify inside him. Vernon Watkins, for instance, wrote that Dylan's 'Poem In October' had been contemplated for all the three unproductive London war years before it was set down finally and sent to Watkins in 1944 from Llangain, Dylan's old haunt by Fern Hill and by his dead aunt's farm. Even when he was temporarily free of debt or concern, which was rare enough, Dylan showed no great urge to write more poetry; in fact, the pressures upon him may well have contributed to the coming of the poems, while his enjoyable paid work on other forms of words may have aided the actual forming of the lines of verse. All writing of whatever sort interpenetrates and informs all other writing from the same pen. No author can put his different styles of words into little boxes; they spill over. Dylan was a genius both at poetry and at prose, and his waste of words was chiefly in his conversation, not from his pen. His whole life enriched his later and greater poems.

Dylan grew more and more to be the family man now, and Caitlin's portrait of him was illuminating. He remained very much the uncontrollable child, even with his children. He would flood Caitlin with torrents of words, since there was no fury like the weak against the weak. Because of his Welsh hypochondrias, which he wanted lovingly nursed and spoiled, he hated real illness in his own children, because they sprang from him and seemed tainted by him. "He was never his proper self till there was something wrong with him; and, if ever there was a danger of him becoming 'whole', which was very remote, he would crack another of his chicken bones, without delay, and wander happily round in his sling, piling up plates with cucumber, pickled onions, tins of cod's roe, boiled sweets; to push into his mouth with an unseeing hand, as they came, while he went on solidly reading his trash."

Caitlin admitted that Dylan was better than she was at living the simple, or moronic, life. She thought it was because he was literally "out of this world". His habits had hardly changed from his adolescent Swansea days, when his own mother had been his early Caitlin in the arranging of him. Late out of bed, early to the lunchtime pub. Back to a heavy lunch, eaten apart from the children and their noise. Then away to a shed or an office, "and bang into intensive scribbling, muttering, whispering, intoning, bellowing and juggling of words; till seven o'clock prompt" and it was opening-time in the pubs all over Wales and the British Isles.

The one worm that gnawed at Dylan's innards and swallowed his muse was debt. Here again, Caitlin understood and could not help. She herself liked no more to look for a job than Dylan did; her work was the children and the nursing of him; his puritanism, anyway, would

Dylan and Caitlin in 1946.

have prevented him from allowing her to go out to find work to support them all. In temperament also, despite the appearances, Dylan cared more about money than Caitlin did. "Poor nervous Dylan, who had inherited, besides his father's hypochondria, his acid pessimism for always anticipating the worst, suffered sleepless nights more than me. I had developed, through never having any, and my mother's lofty teaching, that it is vulgar to speak of money, a happy detachment from it, and, though nobody enjoyed the spending of it more, it was a solemn duty with me, yet I could never make myself feel it really mattered, or appreciate the value of it. And of course it was Dylan had the job of making it."

With such a carefree and careless attitude to money in his wife, and with little talent for keeping any of it himself, Dylan was doomed to mounting debts and occasional excesses. Caitlin recognised that the lack of moderation and love of racketing waste in both of them was fatal. They always lived in hope of a mystical lump of money, which never came to solve all their problems. In the interim, they drank in the evenings to forget their problems, and they took out the frustrations of their lives in their attacks on each other.

This is the part of Dylan's married life which was so frequently misunderstood, and which led to the view of many of Dylan's friends that Caitlin and marriage prevented him from fulfilling himself as a poet. They often had murderous quarrels in public as well as in private. It seemed to outsiders that this violence and shrewishness on the part of his wife destroyed the security Dylan needed to write. In fact, the truth was the opposite. It was because of the security provided first by his mother and then by Caitlin that Dylan managed to write at all: he was a poet of the villa and the family. But the frustrations bred by this dull and simple life, the lunges away from poverty through alcohol, led to a war between the two of them that was the catharsis of all their niggling and monotonous days. Their fights were an essential part of their daily life, "and became fiercer and more deadly at each onslaught, so that you could have sworn no two people reviled each other more; and could never, under any fabulous change of circumstances, come together again." Yet these fights were almost worth while because of the reconciliation which followed, the air clear, love assured, quarrelling indefinitely postponed until the next instalment.

Such were the excesses of Dylan's life on the home front, while the world fought its own battles across the globe. At only one point did the madness of the time intrude into Dylan's domestic strife. To

New Quay in that summer of 1945, an exhausted Commando officer
returned, bringing with him his weapons. He had not been through
the reconstruction camps, set up to make ex-soldiers forget how to kill,
and he found himself in a pacific town which had ignored the hostilities
and saw his courage as a form of brutalism. His wife was a neighbour of
Dylan's and he was jealous of Dylan's presence near her while he had
been away fighting. He began to insult people in the Black Lion, until
Dylan and the other regulars threw him out. That night, his wife and
child fled to the Thomases' bungalow and he followed her, firing a
sten-gun through its asbestos walls, then kicking in the door. Faced
with a maniac and backed by women with babies, Dylan showed a
certain courage. He got the gun away from the ex-Commando, who then
produced a hand-grenade, threatening to blow everybody to kingdom
come unless he got his gun back. Dylan gave him the gun back. This
pacified the raging husband, who went off with his wife and child.

It was a stupid, likely, hysterical episode that mirrored the madness
of the end of the war. Curious, indeed, that there were so few murders
or outbreaks of violence among the millions of trained killers returned
home from their military jobs. 1945 was the year of the unsettling into
peace, and the episode seems to have confirmed Dylan in his first ideas
about the Llareggub of *Under Milk Wood* as a sane lazy town surrounded
by a world gone insane with being at war. He had fled to Wales to
secure his precarious peace. His tooth-and-clawing was reserved for
his beloved enemy, his wife. He was writing his most rural and lyrical
poems in denial of the times. If once the war intruded upon him, he
would exclude it more thoroughly than ever. As he had written again
to T. W. Earp, claiming that not even Donald Taylor and films would
get him out of his sea-side truce:

> It's a long way from London, as the fly bombs,
> And nothing of Donald's guile can lug me
> Away from this Wales where I sit in my combs
> As safe and snug as a bugger in Rugby.
> We've got a new house and it's called Majoda.
> Majoda, Cards, on the Welsh-speaking sea.
> And we'll stay in this wood-and-asbestos pagoda
> Till the black-out's raised on London and on me.

Broadcasting the Word

I do not remember – that is the point – the first impulse that pumped and shoved most of the earlier poems along, and they are still too near to me, with their vehement beat-pounding black and green rhythms like those of a very young policeman exploding, for me to see the written evidence of it. My interpretation of them – if that is not too weighty a word just for reading them aloud and trying to give some idea of their sound and shape – could only be a parroting of the say that I once had.

from 'On Reading One's Own Poems' DYLAN THOMAS

Opposite: *Ink wash drawing of Dylan by Michael Ayrton, 1947.*

Broadcasting the Word

Dylan did not stay in his Majoda by the sea. Living conditions in post-war England seemed so hard and progress so slow that Dylan kept on begging American acquaintances to help him and his family to emigrate across the Atlantic. In July, 1945, he was writing to the American anthologist Oscar Williams, asking him to find a sponsor for the poet's family, whether it were Harvard, *Time* magazine or a rich man. "A patron would do just as well, to say that he will look after me & mine in luxury, New York, or even in a kennel, Texas. I should most like to read, library or lecture at Harvard." Later, he pleaded with his American publisher to bring him over, and then tried for a job with the University of Virginia. These many attempts to reach the United States were the background of his later acceptance of John Malcolm Brinnin's offer of an American lecture tour in 1949. Dylan was not seduced into first crossing the Atlantic; he had been trying to do so for five years. No victim ever went more willingly to his gregarious death by strangers.

While waiting to emigrate, Dylan made makeshift arrangements for living in England. There were small flats in London, friends' hospitality in the country, and finally an odd circular log cabin at the end of the garden of the Oxford historian, A. J. P. Taylor, and his wife Margaret, who was fond of Dylan and took him in to stay for a year. Alcohol and stomach troubles brought Dylan low, but he soon recovered and made regular appearances on the B.B.C., using his sonorous and mellow voice to broadcast his fame as a poet as well as his set pieces.

Two poets and radio producers were particularly Dylan's employers and drinking companions during his first period with the B.B.C. The first was the South African Roy Campbell, a most physical and outrageous man, the second was the Irishman Louis MacNeice, who was fastidious and biting. Their pubs were near Langham Place, the Dover Castle and the George and Stag, with the Tavern at Lord's Cricket Ground or the M.L. Club to fill in the drinking gap during closing-time in the afternoons. Here Dylan reproduced the Soho pattern of steady pubbing, seeking work and getting drunk, the centre of a widening circle of the second-rate and the taggers-on of celebrity.

Dylan now wore a continual cigarette on his mouth, and his face and his belly were bloated. His old friend from Swansea, Charles Fisher, has described how Dylan could always be found at the time, if enough bars were combed to trace his willing progress. "Ah. Here is the green man at the height of his acclaim. He sits in a corner propped up by two walls, a smouldering, soggy firework sending up stars of singular lucidity. His admirers surround him. What will he do next? They wonder. Will he burst or explode? A long silence. Dylan moves his head. A dozen necks crane forward to gather crumbs of irreverence or, perhaps, to learn how to write a poem. 'A pint, I say', he rumbles in that deep belly-voice that makes audiences shiver. The pint is quickly fetched."

So the *enfant terrible* grew into the *célébrité choquant*. Dylan played his role of performer and poet more morosely now, as the accumulating alcohol slowed his responses and darkened his perceptions. He was less ready to suffer fools gladly, although always willing to take another drink from them. Rosalind Wade had first met the young poet in 1934 and had found in him the elementary desire to shock, "rather as a certain type of child will scribble on a clean wall." Then, he had attacked everything and everybody, "interlarding his comments with any and every swear word," but he had totally failed to disrupt the carefully-tolerant liberal gathering in evening dress through which he had sat like a malignant gnome. By 1946, however, when she met him again at a literary dinner, he came under protest and went out to get a drink, unable to bear the chit-chat before eating. "This horror of formality and small talk was an utterly genuine reaction. Finally he reappeared and sat through the meal, throwing pellets of bread at the other diners. But when the 'talk' began it was good to see his boredom and indifference drop like a mask from his face, as he listened attentively to every word and afterwards congratulated the speaker with spontaneous enthusiasm. It was in this mood that he delivered commentaries and broadcasts, once the crust of resentment and seeming rudeness had been broken through."

The way Dylan lived between the casual evenings and bedrooms of London and the precarious cheek-by-jowl cottage with his family at Oxford caused a rapid worsening of his health. He alternated so rapidly between high spirits and collapse that his friends became worried. As

he wrote from Oxford to T. W. Earp, he varied in London from being roaringly well to being a little mewling ruin. But down in the country again with Caitlin, he felt "back in ordinary middle health again, headachy, queasy, feverish, of a nice kind of normal crimson & bilious . . . nearly well enough not to have to go out in the morning in order to feel well enough to work this afternoon."

So the process of city deterioration and country recuperation was beginning to accelerate. The fault and the wages lay in Dylan's job. The B.B.C. was a proud and jealous and penny-pinching organisation. It looked after its own, it was clubby, and it did not pay well. Dylan broadcast about once a week during his year at Oxford, including many of the radio pieces collected in *Quite Early One Morning*. In his preface to this collection, Dylan's Welsh producer, Aneirin Talfan Davies, testified that Dylan's reading of his own poems increased his influence as a poet. The bardic tradition, by which a poet chanted his own verses, suited Dylan particularly well, as he enjoyed his rich performance, even if he knew of the pitfalls of exaggeration. He declared himself one of the dangerous group of readers-aloud of his own poems who managed "to mawken or melodramatize them, making a single simple phrase break with the fears or throb with the terrors from which he deludes himself the phrase has been born."

Yet such is the power of Thomas's recorded voice that it now is impossible to separate the hearing of his poems from the sound of him reading them. There was a magnificence and a resonance in the voice of the man which reverberates in the memory. However well others may read the poems, Dylan's own voice seems to superimpose itself over all, making other versions inadequate. In that way, he answered his own self-doubts about the indulgence of serving as his own bard on the most popular medium of his time. As he mused on the air:

> Reading one's own poems aloud is letting the cat out of the bag. You may have always suspected bits of a poem to be over-weighted, overviolent, or daft, and then, suddenly, with the poet's tongue around them, your suspicion is made certain. How he slows up a line to savour it, remembering what trouble it took, once upon a time, to make it just so, at the very moment, you may think, when the poem needs crispness and speed. Does the cat snarl or mew the better when its

Opposite: *Roy Campbell*

143

> original owner – or father, even, the tom-poet – let it out of
> the bag, than when another does, who never put it in?

This tom-poet did. Certain of his readings became internationally famous. The Third Programme only gave a small audience for his poetry readings, both from his own poems and from those of other poets such as Wilfred Owen and Sir Philip Sidney and Henry Vaughan and Edward Thomas. But his prose pieces of reminiscence were repeated again and again, for the rich phrases and humour and joy of them, the quality of grand nostalgia for all the Christmases rolling "down the hill towards the Welsh-speaking sea, like a snowball growing whiter and bigger and rounder, like a cold and headlong moon bundling down the sky that was our street." That large and bell-sounding voice was like the tones of the favourite uncle, who made that faraway time of long ago seem more full of plums and cackles and brandy than the nowadays.

Aneirin Talfan Davies declared that Dylan was aware of the dangers of his noble style of delivery, sometimes calling himself "a second-rate Charles Laughton". But, in fact, he so enjoyed his performances that his running-down of his style only seems like false modesty. He was never pompous, if he was sometimes exaggerated; he was never untrue to the words, if he did sometimes inflate their emotive strength. Davies never forgot Dylan's own reading of the closing liturgical lines from 'Ceremony After A Fire Raid', when he thundered out from an oversized jacket and a vast expanse of rumpled shirt the lines:

> The masses of the sea under
> The masses of the infant-bearing sea
> Erupt, fountain, and enter to utter for ever
> Glory, glory, glory
> The sundering ultimate kingdom of genesis' thunder.

Frequent broadcasting also refined in Dylan what documentary screen-writing had begun to do, the need to be clear for a mass audience. Dylan himself declared on the radio that it was impossible to be too clear. Sensitive as he was to all criticism, accusations of wilful obscurity hurt Dylan the most, for it was his worst fault. The very complexities of his style caused it to tangle from time to time, and it took him many

Opposite: *The poet and radio producer Louis Macneice, in the Stag's Head, Hallam Street, near to the BBC.*

private intonings and some public utterings to undo the knots in some of his poems. Chanting and shouting his verses made them alive to him. As he wrote of a Festival of Spoken Poetry, "Known words grow wings; print springs and shoots; the voice discovers the poet's ear; it's found that a poem on a page is only half a poem."

Naturally, Dylan's reputation grew slowly. In January, 1947, he wrote to his parents from Oxford and mentioned a broadcast which he had delivered on 'Tonight's Talk' after the news bulletin. He declared that a lot of people had found the talk eccentric; it certainly was not what most people expected to hear after the news. He had received quite a big post from it, "half of it enthusiastic, the other half calling me anything from obscurantist to poseur, surrealist comedian to Bedlamite." In these salad days of his wireless work, Dylan still had to accustom a wider audience to his particularities, profound or comic though they were.

This letter also talks of his best radio piece of the period, *Return Journey*, which was eventually first broadcast on the 15th of June, 1947. This autobiographical coming home of the prodigal son to Swansea was produced by Philip Burton, and is Dylan's city counterpart to the later *Under Milk Wood*. For Dylan could now recognise the deep and abiding influence that the comfortable villa'd Welsh halfway city still had upon him. His return to it, though, is suffused with the notice of change and the approval of death. Two physical metamorphoses had taken place – the frog-goggling boy had become the heavy man, and German bombers had blitzed the heart of Swansea for three days, making rubble of many of its familiar landmarks. So old Dylan searched for his lost youth through the ruins of his birthplace under a snow-blanket on a wild February morning, walking by the "fish-frailed, netbagged, umbrella'd, pixie-capped, fur-shoed, blue-nosed, puce-lipped, blinkered like drayhorses, scarved, mittened, galoshed, wearing everything but the cat's blanket, crushes of shopping-women crunched in the little Lapland of the once grey drab street", only for the search to end in Cwmdonkin Park with the keeper saying that young Dylan was dead.

Warm and elegiac, yearning for the past that could never come again, Dylan found his true prose voice in the broadcasting of it. For this whole year, he hardly wrote a poem. The B.B.C. had most of him, certainly the best of him, and paid him too little for his labour. The files

Opposite: *Dylan Thomas in about 1946.*

146

Dylan Thomas gives a poetry reading on the radio in about 1947.

of the B.B.C. are full of Dylan's requests for money, failure to produce commissioned work, quarrels with the accounting department. In one issue of the *Listener* after Dylan's death, Alan Rees went through the files and found a hilarious story of begging on one side and niggling on the other. But the refrain is the same to the end of the final silencing of that resounding voice. "*And,* if it *is* possible to get a little money soon," Dylan wrote pleading to one of his producers, "could it be got,

148

A BBC broadcast in 1949. Left to right: *Vernon Watkins, John Prichard, Alfred Janes, John Griffiths* (standing), *Daniel Jones, and Dylan Thomas.*

somehow, straight, to me, & not through my agents, d'you think? I'm in a hell of a money mess, sued on all sides; trying to finish several things . . . but worried to death; ill with it."

Dylan never made enough to keep himself and his family. Margaret Taylor was their great benefactor at this time and for the next four years, when she capped her charity by buying the Thomas family the Boat House at Laugharne. In 1946, however, she gave them the use of her log cabin in the Oxford garden and Dylan the use of a caravan to write in peace. Her historian husband soon grew tired of the noise of the Thomas family and of Caitlin's and Dylan's continual requests for money. But Margaret Taylor had money of her own, and she conceived her role as a patroness to the poet. As he usually drank away his earnings from broadcasting in London before he made his way back to Oxford, Mrs Taylor was continually helping Caitlin with the house-keeping. This added to Caitlin's resentment of the situation, to have to accept both the frequent absences of her husband and the charities of his friend. In the end, she quarrelled with Margaret Taylor, biting the hand that fed her for fear it might pat her on the head.

Abroad

I think England is the very place for a fluent and fiery writer.
The highest hymns of the sun are written in the dark. I like the
grey country. A bucket of Greek sun would drown in one colour
the crowds of colours I like trying to mix for myself out of a grey
flat insular mud. If I went to the sun I'd just sit in the sun; that
would be very pleasant but I'm not doing it, and the only necessary
things I do are the things I am doing.

from a letter to Lawrence Durrell by Dylan Thomas, December, 1938

The Boat House at Laugharne.

Abroad

The first time Dylan ever left the British Isles was in the spring of 1947 before he settled finally at Laugharne. Using the travelling scholarship from the Society of Authors, he went with his family and with Caitlin's sister and small son first to the Italian Riviera, and then on to a villa outside Florence. There, "the pooled ponded rosed goldfished arboured lizarded swinghung towelled winetabled Aeronshrill garden" led to "a Niobe's eisteddfod of cypresses." Despite the cries of the children, Dylan found some sort of peace and began to write the most ambitious poem of his life. 'In Country Sleep' was to have been the first of four parts of a major work; in fact, he did complete two parts more, 'Over Sir John's Hill' and 'In The White Giant's Thigh'; the final poem which was to relate all together in a great hymn to the natural universe was unwritten at the time of Dylan's death.

Dylan's intention in the poems was clear to him. All his life, religion had bothered him and the world had dumbfounded him. He could not escape God because of the beauty of His works. As Dylan wrote of the poems in 1951, they were "poems in praise of God's world by a man who doesn't believe in God." There again, that statement was not quite true. Dylan was unwilling to believe in God, but his very thoughts and words and rhythms were suffused with biblical themes and heavenly reverences, for a natural god or God in nature.

> . . . A hill touches an angel. Out of a saint's cell
> The nightbird lauds through nunneries and domes of leaves
> Her robin breasted tree, three Marys in the rays.
> *Sanctum sanctorum* the animal eye of the wood
> In the rain telling its beads, and the gravest ghost
> The owl at its knelling. Fox and holt kneel before blood . . .

Opposite: *Caitlin and Aeronwy in the River Taf at Laugharne.*

If Dylan referred in the poem to the Bible as tales and fables, yet he praised "The saga from mermen to seraphim leaping!" He worshipped legend and God in His legends, Celtic and Christian. He was the heir and victim to the Welsh sense of music and beauty and sin. As he wrote in 'Over Sir John's Hill' of the estuary of his loved Laugharne:

> It is the heron and I, under judging Sir John's elmed
> Hill, tell-tale the knelled
> Guilt
> Of the led-astray birds whom God, for their breast of whistles,
> Have mercy on,
> God in his whirlwind silence save, who marks the sparrows hail,
> For their souls' song.

These are not lines written by an unbeliever, but by a man slowly won over to what Dylan called in his radio talk on these last poems, "the godhead, the author, the milky-way farmer, the first cause, architect, lamp-lighter, quintessence, the beginning Word, the anthropomorphic bowler-out and blackballer, the stuff of all men, scapegoat, martyr, maker, woe-bearer – He, on top of the hill in heaven, weeps whenever, outside that state of being called his country, one of his worlds drops dead, vanishes screaming, shrivels, explodes, murders itself. And, when he weeps, Light and His tears glide down together, hand in hand." The poems show how, by celestial mercy, the dead earth rises to exult. The ancient myth of the divine destroyer and redeemer is sung again.

Dylan began this "affirmation of the beautiful and terrible worth of the Earth" when he was away from that part of his earth that spoke to him. He was homesick abroad, he travelled badly. He complained from his Italian villa to his English drinking companions: "This pig in Italy bitterly knows – O the tears on his snub snout and the squelch in the trough as he buries his flat, Welsh head in shame, and guzzels and blows – that he should have written, three wine vats gone . . . but with a grunt in the pines, time trottered on! the spirit was willing: the ham was weak. The spirit was brandy: the ham was swilling. And oh the rasher-frying sun! What a sunpissed pig I am not to dip a bristle in Chianti, and write. I have so many excuses, and none at all."

Dylan always did have too many and no excuses. His new reason for not writing was the shift from beer to wine, from cloud to sun, so that his face flamed scarlet from the exposure to both. He did not get on too well with the young intellectuals of Florence, finding them a

Dylan Thomas in 1947.

damp lot. Unless he clowned more than usual, playing Tarzan, cracking nuts with his teeth and falling in the pond, he could not break through the barrier of language. He thought himself witty in Italian, but this was Italian courtesy; he thought himself violent in behaviour, but Italian descriptions of him show him morose and silent, talking little, "preferring gestures of comprehension or dissent, remaining isolated within his own solitude." His bar was the Café Giubbe Rosse, where he would accept and offer drinks and have to remain largely dumb. Only Stephen Spender was in Florence to add to the British literary circle, and Dylan found his presence sad. "He is on a lecture tour," Dylan wrote of Spender. "He is bringing the European intellectuals together. It is impossible. He said in a lecture I saw reported: 'All poets speak the same language.' It is a bloody lie: who talks Spender?"

The distance from home, however, increased Dylan's love of it. He might have been in exile, so much did he long to get back. 'In Country Sleep' sings with the nostalgia for what he remembered, while his letters complain of the bloodiness of being away. "I am awfully sick of it here, on the beautiful hills above Florence," he wrote to T. W. Earp, "drinking chianti in our marble shanty, sick of vini and contadini and bambini, and sicker still when I go, bumby with mosquito bites, to Florence itself, which is a gruelling museum." His was no Grand Tour, but a continual torment about having to be cultured and away. He could even mock at his own condition, as always:

> In a shuttered room I roast
> Like a pumpkin in a serra
> And the sun like buttered toast
> Drips upon the classic terra,
> Upon swimming pool and pillar,
> Loggia, lemon, pineclad pico,
> And this quite enchanting villa
> That isn't worth a fico,
> Upon terrace and frutteto
> Of this almost a palazzo
> Where the people talk potato
> And the weather drives me pazzo . . .

At the end of July, Dylan absconded with his family to Elba where it was even hotter, but he was happier being at the sea-side with children, no Swansea beach, but an inferno where he could hardly hold a pen for the blisters on his hands, the waterfall of sweat in his eyes and the peeling of his rainsoft skin, as he sat on his "Sing-Sing-hot-seat" in his hotel. Back he scrambled to Oxfordshire in mid-August, never to return abroad with his family again.

He did, however, go to Prague in 1949 to help inaugurate the Communist Writers' Union. Dylan was not a member of the Communist Party, although many of his Fitzrovia drinking-companions had carried the card in the 1930s, before the Stalin 'purge' trials and the attack on Poland with Hitler had made orthodox Communism stink in the nostrils of many of the more literary Party members. Neither was Dylan a fellow-traveller; for he did travel badly with any formal or foreign doctrine. On the other hand, he was a sympathiser with the aims of Communism, for no contemporary political doctrine declared more noble principles in the struggle of humanity against the evils of industrialism and capitalism. If the practice of Communism was often shoddy, well, the spirit was willing: the ham was weak – as in the pig masters of George Orwell's *Animal Farm*.

If Dylan had any political label, he must have been classified as a romantic Socialist, entirely for his own advantage, yet with freedom for all. He wanted his basic money problems taken over by the State so that he could choose to write without financial pressure. Another of his answers to the *Horizon* questionnaire of 1946 on 'The Cost of Letters' was specific on this key point of a libertarian welfare society: "The State should do no more for writers than it should do for any other person who lives in it. The State should give shelter, food, warmth, etc., whether the person works for the State or not. Choice of work, and the money that comes from it, should then be free for that man; what work, what money, is his own bother." For these reasons, whatever clandestine political motive there may have been, Dylan would sign documents such as the Stockholm Peace Petition and the Rosenberg Petition, which his disillusioned ex-Communist friends would not touch.

When in Prague, Dylan chose to remain in his jovial blinkers, the snowy and Kafkaesque world of that city rosy-pink in his view. He evaded the issue of the censorship of Czech writers by taking to beer and Slivovice and personal answers. When one Czech writer and translator told him that it was impossible to publish modern poetry in Prague at the time, he replied that publishing did not matter. He would take a job in Prague, if he had to, and write as he wished. "A real poet must stand everything and it doesn't matter if he publishes or not." His real friend there was a cheery ex-Surrealist called Vitezslav Nezval, whose boisterous jokes and drinking with Dylan seem to have been one of the causes for his political disgrace during the Official Writers' Congress, so that he was forbidden to deliver his speech at the final session of it. This governmental act somewhat disillusioned Dylan, but he stepped clear of the pack-ice of the Cold War and in his speech to the Congress he merely declared that he was a Welsh poet, who had no other wish than to write poems, but unfortunately who had to work to live. Then he sincerely

Overleaf: *Back in Wales* ". . . am I the same person, sadly staring over the flat, sad, estuary sands . . ."

conveyed the genuine friendship of all English and Welsh writers to any writers' organisation that owned both a daily paper and its own magazine.

Rather like the jesting Pilate, Dylan did not stay in Prague for an answer to the only relevant questions – If there is a writers' organisation, who can belong to it, what may be published by it? Dylan had the freedom to return to Wales and that he did. His only trip to a Communist-governed state was a holiday and an irrelevance to him, proving him to be as apolitical as he sometimes claimed to be.

If neither Italy nor Czechoslovakia had any great influence on Dylan, his first lecture tour to America did. It was the fatal plunge into an inclusive and destructive world. An admirer of his, the poet and critic John Malcolm Brinnin, had been trying for some years to arrange for Dylan to make a lecture tour because he had been part of Brinnin's consciousness for over a decade. Brinnin was not successful in his purpose until he was appointed the director of the Poetry Centre of the Young Men's and Young Women's Hebrew Association in New York. That such a body should become the sponsor of the leading Celtic poet was odd, although Brinnin declared that his only reason for accepting the job was to invite Dylan across the Atlantic. However that might be, Dylan was invited for two well-paid poetry readings. The Welsh poet immediately accepted, for the United States remained his promised and golden land. He asked Brinnin to fix up more paid lectures for him. Brinnin now accepted, becoming Dylan's lecture agent and much more, his "reluctant guardian angel, brother's keeper, nursemaid, amanuensis, bar companion." In fact, Brinnin was to do none of these jobs well enough, for he himself was too involved with Dylan and certainly not strongly angelic enough to guard Dylan from his demons of drink and smothering by strangers.

Yet on that first tour, Dylan's strut into the fond and deadly embrace of the United States was begun. Brinnin's book, *Dylan Thomas in America*, is its record. All he says seems true; what he does not say howls between the lines. Dylan was evidently devastated by Manhattan, "this Titanic dream world, soaring Babylon, everything monstrously rich and strange." He immediately took refuge in some of the seedier Irish bars of Third Avenue and particularly in the White Horse Tavern, "as homely and dingy as many a London pub, and perhaps just as old." And he immediately began to confound and alarm the inhibited Brinnin,

Opposite: *John Malcolm Brinnin with Dylan in Millbrook, N.Y. in 1952.*

appalled that the "purest lyrical poet of the twentieth century" should live a discrepancy "between the disciplines of art and the consolations of liquor, bar-room garrulity, encounters with strangers, and endless questing for meaningless experience." Poor Dylan. Poor Brinnin, wanting both to take care of his hero and impose sanity upon him, also wanting to get rid of him and his self-devouring miseries. Brinnin was no Caitlin, to bluff out Dylan and control him. For Brinnin was a righteous puritan, who could not understand or command a Dylan, still playing at Sam Bennet in this cornucopia of free liquor from the easily impressed, still playing the Swansea hard innocent with an "ability neither to reject nor to accept, neither wholly to go nor to stay." As Caitlin knew, if Dylan could get away with the responsibility for his excesses by appearing to have them put upon him, he would do so. For then he could excuse his Welsh conscience and sense of sin; it was not him, it was the others. Some are born drunks, some achieve drunkenness, but Dylan liked to have drunkenness thrust upon him. This America liked to do, and Brinnin could not stop it.

The result was that this first lecture tour of three months was a roaring success, or roaring and a success. Dylan lived up to his roistering and shocking reputation, while turning in some of his greatest performances as a lecturer. Brinnin tells of him before the first lecture, when Dylan was sick and vomiting blood. Yet at the right time he walked on the stage, "shoulders straight, chest out in his staunch and pouter-pigeon advance", and proceeded to give the first of those performances which Brinnin thought were to bring to America a whole new conception of poetry reading. Yeats, Hardy, Auden, Lawrence, MacNeice, Alun Lewis, Edith Sitwell, and finally his own poems were Dylan's repertoire, and he received ovations from the people who packed the auditorium. He did seem the fat Rimbaud come again, Villon and more, the romantic poet in his ecstasy and agony. And his poems were those of genius, too.

Karl Shapiro has written of Dylan's presence creating his impossible audience, "a general audience for a barely understandable poet." To express his poems, Dylan did not have to clarify them. He became a producer of himself, a clown at his own tragedy, the dramatist of himself as a poet. For his audience understood him as a mob understands its leader without necessarily taking in his words. His listeners were probably "the first nonfunereal poetry audience in fifty years, an audience that had been deprived of poetry by fiat." Dylan set them

Opposite: *Dylan in the White Horse Tavern, New York, in 1952.*

alive by his voice of elation and anguish ringing over their heads. "They know it is acting. They know this is poetry and they know it is for them."

Dylan certainly knew of his power over his hearers. After one early lecture in London, he complained of his own character as a lecturer. "I detest the humility I should have, and am angry when I am humble. I appreciate the social arrogance I have in the face of my humility." Dylan felt he had to be peacock-proud in his public character, while wanting to have the attractive modesty of the confident and the famous. He could never forget how hardly he had made his way; he wanted to hide his lack of knowledge of the world by flaunting his power of words and cock-sure attack on anything superior. Even more brash than the poor boy made good is the suburban poet notorious outside his own town. If prophets and poets are without honour in their own country, they are stuffed with it abroad.

Photograph of W. H. Auden pinned to the wall of Dylan's tool-shed at Laugharne.

Of course, Dylan knew of his deliberate degradation of himself and his talents, once he was sent back home, sodden with liquor and with very little profit in his pocket. His judgement on this killing process across the Atlantic was made on the B.B.C. just before his death from it, willy and nilly as it was. Because Dylan voluntarily accepted to go, he would never condemn his host as his murderer. For he was the swilling victim, the jester at the massacre of his own self. He laughed at the little English writers of tiny reputation at home, suddenly become gods in Manhattan and beyond, and he would not bite the hand that filled his glass. He was too generous for that pub blasphemy.

See the garrulous others, also, gabbing and garlanded from one nest of culture-vultures to another: people selling the English way of life and condemning the American way as they swig and guzzle through it; people resurrecting the theories of surrealism for the benefit of remote parochial female audiences who did not know it was dead, not having ever known it had been alive; people talking about Etruscan pots and pans to a bunch of dead pans and wealthy pots in Boston. And there, too, in the sticky thick of lecturers moving across the continent black with clubs, go the foreign poets, catarrhal troubadours, lyrical one-night-standers, dollar-mad nightingales, remittance-bards from at home, myself among them booming with the worst.

Dylan mocked at his own slow wasting, quickening in America. He was only at home at home, yet his restless years drove him abroad, as if he knew he would rather finish himself than his greatest poem. As Samuel Beckett once wrote, sometimes the only thing is to be done, to have done.

Taf estuary, Laugharne.

Laugharne and Away

And now that I am back in Wales, am I the same person, sadly staring over the flat, sad, estuary sands, watching the herons walk like women poets, hearing the gab of gulls, alone and lost in a soft kangaroo pocket of the sad, salt West, who once, so very little time ago, trundled under the blaring lights, to the tune of cabhorns, his beautiful barrow of raspberries.

. . . I know that I am home again because I feel just as I felt when I was not at home, only more so.

from 'Living in Wales' a broadcast by Dylan Thomas on 23rd June, 1949

Laugharne and Away

One of the signs of a species about to become extinct is that it fouls its own nest. It is also the sign of a man who has no will to live. Dylan, on the other hand, never fouled his own nest at home in Laugharne, where he did want to live. Testimony is still unanimous there. Although many of the townspeople felt after his death he had ridiculed them in *Under Milk Wood*, none thought of him as rather more than one of them. In fact, they seemed to put him much on the level of a workman, for he dressed and behaved like one and drank in the pub with other workmen. He stuck to beer, he never caused a scandal, he was faithful to Caitlin, he paid his bills in the end, he was a good neighbour in house and pub in a most conservative town – "true bloody blue to the core", as Dylan called it, "even the workers vote Liberal and as for listening to a word against *dear* Winston . . ."

Even drink was no problem to Dylan when he felt secure and at home. He was very specific about this to his patroness, the Princess Caetani, who kept on sending him money for the first draft of *Under Milk Wood*, eventually to be printed in her private magazine, *Botteghe Oscure*. Dylan wrote from Laugharne that he was frightened of drink too, but only when he was whirlingly perplexed and magnified his ordinary troubles into monsters.

> When I am here, or anywhere I like, and am busy, then drink's no fear at all and I'm well, terribly well, and gay, and unafraid and full of other nicer nonsenses, and altogether a dull, happy fellow only wanting to put into words, never into useless, haphazard, ugly, unhappy action, the ordered turbulence, the ubiquitous and rinsing grief, the unreasonable glory, of the world I know and don't know.

If, then, Dylan was so frightened of drink and self-destruction when he was away from home, why did he go on the four successive lecture tours of America that were to culminate in his death? An answer seems to lie in his quick powers of recovery once he reached anchor and Caitlin at Laugharne again, a feeling that he would always be able to recuperate in Wales, however unsteady his progress abroad. In one letter to American friends, he begged to be remembered, "round, red, robustly raddled, a bulging Apple among poets, hard as nails made of cream cheese, gap-toothed, balding, noisome, a great collector of dust and a magnet for

Dylan plays nap in the bar with Ivy Williams, proprietress of Brown's Hotel in Laugharne.

moths, mad for beer, frightened of priests, women, Chicago, writers, distance, time, children, geese, death, in love, frightened of love, liable to drip." He went on fondly about his final liquid, libidinous fortnight in New York, and declared that, as a result, he had never felt physically better in his life with a spring in his step and a song in his gut "and poems to write and no need to hurry to write them." He wrote that he had to ruin his health again because he felt so preposterously well.

Such were the healing joys of Laugharne – and of love. For as Dylan found his family refuge, so he put the first real strain on his relationship with Caitlin, although a second son Colm had been born to them. In New York, Dylan had met and fallen in love with a dark sophisticated handsome woman, a professional publishing executive who was the antithesis of all that Dylan apparently liked. His sexual triumph over such a *Vogue* woman persuaded Dylan that he was in love with her as well as Caitlin. She came to England and went with him on an illicit week-end to Brighton. Caitlin got to hear of it through the traditional grey good friend. In this miserable confrontation of loves and loyalties, Caitlin won a slow and grudged and bitter victory, while the American woman accepted the end of the affair a year later, "with all its soap-opera bubbles broken, finally."

Caitlin insisted upon it. When the choice came, Dylan knew where his strength and the source of his poetry lay, his only stability in the racketing waste of his life. Briefly he went to Iran to work on a documentary about the oil business, and from the lonely and puritan hotels there, he wrote love-letters to his Caitlin, his Cattleanchor, his dear, without whom he could not live. In the accelerating process of his rush from health to ruin, Dylan knew that he could not sever his only rope that tied him to his true work. Without her, "the bloody animal" did always go on. Yet with her at Laugharne, the poet could work.

So Caitlin took him back to home and children in the summer of 1951. Dylan faced up to the facts of his being, his relationship with his family and his parents. His father was now dying, and Dylan was shocked into his last fertile period of writing poetry whenever he was free from the nervous hag that rode him "biting and scratching into insomnia, nightmare, and the long anxious daylight." Dylan's poem on his father dying was his own valedictory; it spoke of his own refusal to give way to his deteriorating health and abuse of his peace of mind. As much as he

Opposite: *Dylan at a New York bar "... round, red, robustly raddled, a bulging Apple among poets ..."*

was his father's son, he would rage, rage against the dying of the light.

> Wild men who caught and sang the sun in flight,
> And learn, too late, they grieved it on its way,
> Do not go gentle into that good night . . .

He could not show his father this poem about the old man's dying yet, but he could write both his own celebration of his own birthday, "his driftwood thirty-fifth wind turned age", and his own 'Lament' for his repetitive contrasts of life, which he knew were killing him and which he could not stop. The old ram rod of the five verses of the poem is dying of women, dying of bitches, dying of welcome, dying of downfall, and finally dying of strangers. Dylan knew the causes of his unease and his chosen way of death.

Brinnin came to Laugharne to tempt Dylan back to America again. Caitlin did not want him to go, but, in the end, accepted on condition that she could go as well. In the interval before going, she moved with Dylan to London briefly, so that he could make some money from broadcasting there. It was a trough in his fame and life, the year before his *Collected Poems* and later *Under Milk Wood* were to make him an international success, acknowledged as the leading British poet of his generation. His old drinking companions found him sad now, restless, more morose and sullen in his thorough drinking. To one hearer, he looked "like a transcendental tinplate worker", but to himself, his old tough façade was cracking. As he told an American critic, he should have been what he was over twenty years before, "arrogant and lost. Now I am humble and found. I prefer the other."

That second running away from Laugharne to the lecture-circuit masterminded by Brinnin was even more outrageous and self-destroying than the first tour. Dylan was hardly loath to go and squander himself, prodding Brinnin to "put out feelers, spin wheels, grow wings" for him. Brinnin duly did, meeting Caitlin and Dylan off the *Queen Mary* on the 20th January, 1952, with a square of red carpet in his hand. It was the best welcome that Dylan had. For Caitlin proved an impossible companion on the lecture tour, merely adding to the strain of the lionising of Dylan by making scandals in order to bring herself to his notice. To Brinnin, the loud and stormy scenes at parties proved that their marriage was essentially a state of rivalry; they had each other in a death-grip; Dylan's success in America was yet more weight on the cross that Caitlin had to bear. She could not stand being his camp-follower in America, where she was even more estranged from that private inclusive life with him, for which she fought for both of their sakes.

Caitlin's version of the trip was hardly the same. She said that she did not resent for a minute Dylan's success. She admitted the impossibility of not being won over by the adulation poured like hot fudge on Dylan and on her, by extension. She confessed herself overwhelmed by its sticky syrup, until she was left a soulless lump of inarticulate meat. "So what can Dylan have felt like, in spite of his incredible resistance, and amazingly quick recovery powers? One moment he was flat out, in utter self-abandonment, coughing and heaving up his heart, down to the soles of his boots; the next, dolled up, like a puppy's supper, dapper and spruce, or as near as he could get to it. But there was always a grotesque flaw in the tailor's dummy, which,

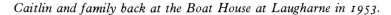

Caitlin and family back at the Boat House at Laugharne in 1953.

177

John Malcolm Brinnin at Laugharne, arranging Dylan's next trip to America.

if I mentioned, I was slaughtered; and if I did not I was blamed for not being interested. Jocularly joking, as though that other prostrate negation, parody of a romantic poet in tubercular convulsions, had no connection with the narrow world, with him. Then nervously twitching and acrimoniously nagging me, about tiny petty things, which neither of us took seriously; but which outsiders were alarmed into thinking was at least the breaking up of our marriage. But our marriage was not a cobweb house drifting on sand; and we enjoyed the back chat, if nobody else did." The scenes were mainly the product of sexual jealousy, he of her, she of him. Thus, in a way, the scandals were proof of their love, although they got dangerously near to the killing of one another in those bloodthirsty vengeances.

The public readings of Dylan, however, merely inflated his reputation, while the whispers of scandal made faculty after literary club ready to endure a Thomas private quarrel in order to feed on the gossip for years afterwards. The only way out of a succession of dull hotel bedrooms and interminable journeys from lecture to lecture lay in the bottle for both of them. America seemed a vast continental party in a lost alien city; there was no relief from the strain. At last, in Arizona, Dylan sent a postcard to Dan Jones from the Tuzigoot stone, one of America's minor ancient monuments. On it, he wrote an epitaph of Caitlin and himself:

> We were killed in action, Manhattan Island, Spring, 1952,
> in a gallant battle against American generosity.
> An American called Double Rye shot Caitlin to death.
> I was scalped by a Bourbon.
> Posthumous love to you . . .

The bottle-scarred Thomases were shipped home with precious little pay to show for being loudly lost in America with their "luggage of dismays . . . peddling and bawling to adolescents the romantic agony of the dead." They simply could not keep any money in their hands. They were too concerned with saving themselves to save any cash. And back at Laugharne, they found their debts greater, the income tax men pressing, Llewelyn turned away from school for failure to pay the fees. Dylan, too, had a succession of illnesses, pleurisy, bronchitis, and gout. Still, he managed to finish the final draft of the 'Prologue' for his

Collected Poems, the most intricate of all his verses. For the first line rhymes with the last, which is also the 102nd line; the second line rhymes with the 101st, while the middle two lines rhyme with each other. Its labyrinth of perfection was so complex and wrought that Dylan seemed to be proving that he still had complete mastery over his art, however much he was wasting the embers of his life.

In fact, even his drinking in pubs was part of his working method at Laugharne. He would suddenly stop his gab for long enough to tear off the end of a cigarette packet, jot down a phrase and stuff the piece of paper in his pocket for later use, if he could find it again in the jumble of his trousers. In the afternoons, he would retire to a tool shed a few hundred yards from the Boat House and work at a table by a stove, a bookcase, and a window looking out over the estuary. Discarded lines and verses and phrases littered the floor about his feet. Once, just before his last trip to America, a neighbour found scraps of a poem torn into little pieces and lying in the lane. She tried to put the scraps together and failed. It was probably a draft for his final unfinished poem on the death of his father.

At the end of the year, just after the publication of Dylan's *Collected Poems* when the son had finally proved himself to be the great poet the father had always wanted to be, D. J. Thomas died on the words, "It's full circle now." In his final years, he had come close to Dylan and had learned to admire his son. They would do crosswords and drink an evening pint together in Brown's Hotel. At his father's cremation, Dylan vomited. His last unfinished poem was to the old man's memory and was discovered by Vernon Watkins. It contained the lines about God and Dylan's father:

> I am not too proud to cry that He and he
> Will never never go out of my mind.
> All his bones crying, and poor in all but pain,
>
> Being innocent, he dreaded that he died
> Hating his God, but what he was was plain:
> An old kind man brave in his burning pride.
>
> The sticks of the house were his; his books he owned.
> Even as a baby he had never cried;
> Nor did he now, save to his secret wound . . .

Opposite: *Dylan's tool-shed study on Cliff Walk, Laugharne.*

Above and opposite: *Dylan at work in his tool-shed study in 1953.*

With the death of his father, Dylan began more and more to become reckless about his own death. His sister, too, died the next spring. Only his mother was left now, and his wife and three children at Laugharne. His own health was deteriorating more and more, his powers of recovery lessening. He began to suffer from black-outs. Once he fell down unconscious at the bar at Brown's Hotel. The proprietor picked him up. When he came round, he asked how long he had been out. "Two minutes", was the reply. "Oh, it wasn't long that time", he said and ordered another drink as though nothing had happened.

He was more afraid than he appeared to be, and his fears were growing. Again he wrote to the Princess Caetani of his terrors and of his self-awareness of his own psychology, both too coward and too brash by turns. "When I try to explain my fear, the confused symbols grow leaden and a woolly rust creeps over the words. How can I say it? I can't. I can say: One instinct of fear is to try to make oneself as little, as un-noticeable, as possible, to cower, as one thinks, unseen and anonymous until the hunt is past. My fearful instinct is to bloat myself like a frog, to magnify my unimportance, to ring a bell for a name, so that, as I bluster and loom twice my size, the hunt, seeing me monstrous, bays by after different & humbler prey. But that is not what I mean: the symbols have wet-brain, the words have swallowed their tongues."

Money matters still pressed. Debts grew. Children demanded. A wife and a mother had to be fed. Bailiffs threatened. Only another American tour seemed to offer any way out, even if it might prove fatal. Although Dylan knew he could only play the poet there and not make poetry, yet he could live for free and send a little money home. He hated his continual begging for aid and his passion for self-glori-fication; " alms, for the love of writing." He would have to go to America again, not for what Caitlin declared was merely flattery and idleness and infidelity, but for what he called appreciation and dramatic work and friends. He had no choice, or else he did not choose to have a choice. He would leave Laugharne.

Ironically, Dylan's appreciation of Laugharne for the B.B.C. was broadcast at the time that he was lying dangerously ill in an American hospital at the point of death. Still more ironically, it had been recorded by him at the Swansea studios on the same day as his other final radio piece, 'A Visit to America', which he had ended with a vision of New

Opposite: *Dylan Thomas in the graveyard at Laugharne shortly after the death of his father.*

York as "a haven cosy as toast, cool as an icebox, and safe as skyscrapers."

However that might have been in memory, it was not a good prophecy for a Welsh bard. Better his nostalgia for that other axis of his life, that interminably dull estuary at Laugharne as opposed to the fatal megalopolis, a Welsh town so set that longish journeys, of only a few hundred yards, were often undertaken only on bicycles, while privacy was all. Laugharne was enviable for "its minding of its own, strange, business; its sane disregard for haste; its generous acceptance of the follies of others, having so many, ripe and piping, of its own; its insular, feather-bed air; its philosophy of 'It will all be the same in a hundred years' time.'" Faced with the prospect of that magical penny-pinching security and backed by the hope of returning to it, Dylan had to set out for the terminal city.

Opposite: *Brown's Hotel in Laugharne.*

Destroyer and Preserver

*The briefest review of Dylan's emotional life would suggest
that no man was ever more adept in killing what he loved, or
suffered more in the consequence.*

JOHN MALCOLM BRINNIN

*Now I am a man no more no more
And a black reward for a roaring life,
(Sighed the old ram rod, dying of strangers) . . .*

from 'Lament' DYLAN THOMAS

Opposite: *Ancient Druid stones, called a cromlech, in a Welsh wood.*

Destroyer and Preserver

Dylan Thomas had always lived under Milk Wood. Wales was a country of recent cities, and in every suburban Welsh boy hid a nostalgia for a "timeless, mild, beguiling island of a town", which his grandmother still remembered like Mary Ann Sailors as the Chosen Land, and where life was still simple and peaceful and direct. For the boy Dylan, Cwmdonkin Park had been a shadow on the green liberty of Mumbles. For the youth Dylan, Swansea had been neither London nor Laugharne, but a dirty town of a city where small and hardly-known and never-to-be-forgotten people lived and always lost. He had not intended to lose there, so he had left, first for London and the seven deadly sins suggested in the incomplete *Adventures in the Skin Trade*, and afterwards, dying of strangers, he had returned to New Quay and Laugharne and all the deadly virtues of small-town Wales that plagued him to escape once more. Yet he had always carried with him an idea which he had mentioned to Bert Trick in his Swansea days as a reporter, the story of a row of terrace houses at a place called Llareggub, where all the inhabitants came out to blab their dreams and hidden desires.

This idea had grown in Dylan's mind in London and in Laugharne, both of which he had first visited in 1934. A year later, he had written of "the stories of the reverend madmen in the Black Book of Llareggub" in his Surrealist story called 'The Orchards'. And just after the outbreak of the war, when he and Caitlin had been staying with Richard Hughes in Laugharne Castle, he had acted in a local one-act farce called *The Devil among the Skins*. Afterwards, as Richard Hughes recalled in a broadcast on the Third Programme, "we all agreed it was absurd to perform such utter rubbish to so noble an audience as the burgesses of Laugharne. Then Dylan had an idea: 'What Laugharne really needs is a play about well-known Laugharne characters – and get them all to play themselves.'"

The war had intervened and Dylan had gone to live in a bungalow in New Quay during the fall of Germany. Here he had written *Quite Early One Morning*, a sketch of life in a seaside town suspiciously like New Quay, for Aneirin Talfan Davies, his B.B.C. talks producer. Dylan had recorded the programme in his rich rhetoric and the broadcast was successful, despite some adverse comments from the Head of Talks that surfaced many years later, criticising Dylan's "breathless, poetic voice", for the words had not seemed to carry it.

However that was, Dylan's words were a foretaste of *Under Milk Wood*. He spoke of a sun-lit sea-town with the sea "lying down still and green as grass after a night of tar-black howling and rolling." The town was not yet awake, while babies cried in the upper bedrooms of salt-white houses dangling over water, and "miscellaneous retired sea captains emerged for a second from deeper waves than ever tossed their boats, then drowned again" in the big seas of their dreams. Landladies in the "bombasined black of their once spare rooms" remembered "their loves, their bills, their visitors." The town was not yet awake, while the narrator "walked through the streets like a stranger come out of the sea," hearing the terrible and violent dreams of the mild-mannered men and women. Cockcrow and larks called the town awake slowly, and some of the voices began to sound, including:

> . . . I am Mrs Ogmore Pritchard and I want another snooze.
> Dust the china, feed the canary, sweep the drawing-room floor;
> And before you let the sun in, mind he wipes his shoes.

This prelude to *Under Milk Wood* echoed Edgar Lee Masters' *The Spoon River Anthology* with its ideas of dead and living people speaking out their dreams and doings in simple poetry, and in fact one of the last programmes Dylan did for the B.B.C. was on Masters' work. Then again, Dylan was influenced by Thornton Wilder's *Our Town*, a debt which he hardly acknowledged. But he discarded his own first structure for his long radio play, as outlined to Richard Hughes and Constantine Fitzgibbon during the war, and to his Welsh radio producer Philip Burton in 1947 in the Café Royal. Then he had wished to write something called *The Village of the Mad*, in which Llareggub would be put on trial for insanity by an official inspector from the war government. In the course of the trial, the villagers would prove themselves free and feckless and sane in a world gone mad with fighting and regulations, greed and regimentation. Llareggub would end by asking for barbed

wire round it to save its dangerous and infectious happiness from contamination by the rest of the crazy human race.

This plot derived from war and possibly from the fact that a secret weapons establishment was built with its barbed wire and sentries just down the coast from Laugharne on the Pendine Sands, within earshot of Dylan's Boat House. Dylan may have escaped the war physically, but his mind rebelled against his cowardice until he seems to have erected an anarchic love of life into a more human cause than patriotism. As the war's influence ebbed into the slow peace of the early 1950s, so Dylan dropped the structure of *The Village of the Mad* into something similar to his only other long radio play, *Return Journey*. In that, a narrator who was himself, came back to Swansea and heard in the voices of his memory and of the living and of the dead, the accounts of his own past life and adolescent dreams. The narrator tacked up "the snowblind hill, a cat-o'-nine-gales whipping from the sea," to Cwmdonkin Park where dusk was folding it around "like another, darker snow." There the park-keeper remembered the little Thomases by their thousands, just as Captain Cat was to remember his sailors under the waves. They were all "dead . . . dead . . . dead."

So a freer form of *Under Milk Wood* suggested itself to Dylan as he began to work on it after 1949 in Laugharne. Within two years, he confessed to the Countess Caetani of his changed intentions, that he wanted "a piece, a play, an impression for voices, an entertainment out of the darkness of the town I live in." Jobs for quick cash got in the way of Dylan finishing the radio play. Even at its first stage performance in the Young Men's and Young Women's Hebrew Association in New York in 1953, Dylan was said to be still drafting the last revisions to it as he and the other actors went on the stage.

A shorter version, however, called *Llareggub, a Piece for Radio Perhaps*, had already appeared in the Countess Caetani's *Botteghe Oscure* in 1952. This unfinished script had reached the Countess with the declaration that only very special circumstances were preventing Dylan from carrying on with the work every minute of the day. These very special circumstances were, naturally, a shortage of money – Dylan wanted one hundred pounds for the fragment, which was basically half the length of the final play, ending on Captain Cat's line, "Organ Morgan's at it early. You can tell it's spring." Douglas Cleverdon has fully explained the various manuscripts of *Under Milk Wood* up to

Opposite: *Dylan reading in the 'Y' in New York, 1953.*

Caitlin and the family at Laugharne while Dylan was away in America.

the final version given to him for performance by the B.B.C. After Dylan's death, his widow Caitlin sued Cleverdon unsuccessfully for the return of the manuscript, which had been sold; but she lost the case. Certainly, Dylan never received from his play in his lifetime what the manuscript fetched after his burial. But it was broadcast practically without cuts on the Third Programme two months after the poet's death – thirteen words in all were omitted according to Cleverdon, "two tits and a bum".

In a way, the finishing of *Under Milk Wood* was the finishing of Dylan Thomas. He paid for his spoken masterpiece with the stilling of his voice. From its solo performance by Dylan in the Fogg Museum at Harvard on the 3rd of May, 1953, to its fourth stage performance for the Young Men's and Young Women's Hebrew Association on the 25th of October of that year, just before his death on the 9th of November, Dylan was made a lion and made drunk to delirium by his American friends and spongers. "He succumbed", as Caitlin later wrote, "like a mesmerized bait, only in this case a short-legged one, to the multitudinous, scavenging, spawn of America." Only the brief interval of his return to Laugharne for the summer of that last year and only the

Family group at Laugharne in September 1953. Left to right: top, *Dylan, Llewellyn;* sitting, *Aeronwy, Mrs Thomas, Colm, Caitlin.*

restraints of home life made Dylan begin to recover from the temptations of "unflagging, disarming American charm". But even ill-health and Caitlin's fear could not stop him from going back to the success of *Under Milk Wood* and to his final dying of strangers in that concrete world of the mad that the villagers of Llareggub had always wanted to keep to the far side of the barbed wire.

Richard Burton, who was Dylan's friend and drinking companion, played Dylan's role of the First Voice in the B.B.C. recording, the Argo record of it, and finally in the film version of 1971. He told me that he had spoken the words over a thousand times waking and sleeping, and that to him the whole play was about religion, sex and death. Thomas had always seen himself in the role of the tubercular poet; one of his favourite tricks was coughing into his handkerchief because of too many cigarettes, then pretending he was a lunger and that he had brought up blood. Yet both of his radio plays echo with prophecies of his early death. As Caitlin wrote, "Dylan and dying, Dylan and dying, they don't go together; or is it that they were bound to go together; he said so often enough, but I did not heed him."

Under Milk Wood opens with two unexplained voices commenting on the sea-side night town of Llaregyb, politer now in its spelling. These voices are not explained, their connection with the characters of the town unknown. They have the power to conjure up dreams, they know intimately the private lives of all the sleepers in Cockle Row and Coronation Street, they are godlike in their comprehension and devilish in their mockery. They seem like natural spirits of the place, taking us through night and dawn and day and dusk back to the final ambiguous description of Milk Wood itself, no longer as in its first mention a place of wedding dreams, where young girls glide "brides-maided by glow-worms down the aisles of the organ-playing wood," but finally a place of Satan and Eden, lust and innocence, "whose every tree-foot's cloven in the black glad sight of the hunter of lovers," with Polly Garter's voice sounding last of all for the townsfolk:

> But I always think as we tumble into bed
> Of little Willy Wee who is dead, dead, dead.

Dylan was always accused of being a destroyer of others as well as of himself, while Caitlin was given the role of his preserver or his destroyer,

Dylan in the dining-room of the Boat House in 1953.

depending on the point of view. Dylan certainly viewed Caitlin as his preserver, his Sunday wife who bore him angels – "Harpies around me out of her womb!" And she knew how to provide the opposition he needed, "gentle, but firm, constant curbing, and a steady, dull, homely bed of straw to breed his fantasies in." Playing the *enfant terrible* killed him, the urge to shock, to amuse, to drink to the last round and the last crowd. Already on the verge of delirium tremens during those last days in New York, he still had to go on what Scott Fitzgerald called a collegiate drunk, to return to his hotel room with the boast, "I've had eighteen straight whiskies. I think that's the record."

Brinnin's *Dylan Thomas in America* tells of Dylan's dying in harrowing detail without ever telling the root cause of it. To Brinnin, Dylan wants to destroy himself. America is only the excuse for self-destruction. Dylan is deliberately intimate with anybody who approaches him. He is on a perpetual drunken spree even without alcohol. His gaiety is not so much spontaneous as premeditated – at first chosen, then a matter of abandon. Dylan's caricature of himself as "the dollar-mad nightingale" in search of "naked women in wet mackintoshes" is a flight from having to write, from having to earn money for his family, a deliberate suicide of genius for which no other person can be blamed. Brinnin himself is the poet turned agent, worrying over Dylan's airfares and bills. Even in the love-affair with the New York publishing woman, Dylan presents himself jeeringly as a "beer-cheapened hoddy-noddy" with "his sodden bounce, his mis-theatrical-demeanour, the boastful tuppence!"

Dylan loves to shock, to wound, to kill, but he finds himself in the end a puritan, maimed in the gut, killed by his own boozing and indiscretions. Brinnin and his friends even have Caitlin confined in an expensive psychiatric home for her own good as Dylan is dying, because of her wild outbursts and hysteria. As she comes home on a boat with Dylan in his box, she asks herself who was so desirous of having her out of the way as to be responsible for it. She has left New York with her husband's embalmed body, "sodden, limp from indistinguishable hangovers", half-killed by the care of his friends.

Such destroying kindness, such indulgence of self-destruction, such yielding to the excesses of genius for the pleasure of observing them, while privately condemning the same excesses for the preservation of one's own distance and conscience, this is what Caitlin could never forget. She did not try to preserve herself after Dylan's death, but she plunged into his riotings and failed at them, not forgiving the meticulous

Brinnin for his accounts of the money earned, his wariness of the laws of libel, his implication that his behaviour was beyond reproach, while only the poet's was bad. To Caitlin, Brinnin was so visibly sensitive that he made her feel like a rhinoceros rooting in an exquisite bed of flowers. She herself tried to join Dylan in his dying. "Whenever I was being extra bad, I said to myself: if it had been the other way round, Dylan would have been twice as bad. But of course it could not have been the other way round; it was one of those ugly preordained things that *had* to happen this way round. More than that I do not know; but there is no doubt Dylan would have made a better job than me of killing himself: for damnation he has done it has he not?"

Wynford Vaughan Thomas and others tell of Dylan's funeral, which seems a wake as full of mythology as the tales of his exploits in bars and beds. There is the story of the friend in the funeral parlour, who looked down at the poet's painted face, loud suit and carnation in his buttonhole, only to declare, "He would never have been seen dead in it." There is the story of the coffin being met at Southampton Dock by the local under-taker, who took the wrong western road back to Wales and was dis-covered by the police heading towards Cornwall; told of his mistake, he declared, "Nobody said to me this bloody country was forked." Then there was the undignified sight of one or two of Dylan's hangers-on slipping away from the beautiful simple burial ceremony to get back to the Boat House and rifle through the poet's manuscripts before the rest of the mourners returned; luckily one of the trustees of the estate got there first.

In his going as in his living, Dylan was bled dry by interested strangers, even at that final "tame, cup of tea, whisky-nipping, saucepan-domesticated, mingling of the original black beetles, raffish Londoners, and Swansea boys in their best provincial suits . . . all caring according to their means, and class. But caring", as Caitlin wrote, "more than any-body had cared at a funeral since." If that last wake was a boozing affair, it was because Dylan had asked that people should get drunk when he was laid in the Green Banks. It is also a tradition in Wales and at Laugharne that nothing becomes a man so in life as the size of his death. A small funeral means a small life, a large funeral bears testimony to fame. As Edward Vale once wrote, "No matter how shabbily you have lived, you will be respected in Wales when you have become a corpse."

Opposite: *Dylan at a rehearsal of* Under Milk Wood *in a New York apartment in May 1953.*

Yet after he had outlived his adolescent preoccupation with an early and Keatsian death, Dylan did not want to commit suicide, by drink or anything else. Brinnin claims that in New York Dylan said that he wanted to die. But this was spoken in broken health and alcoholic melancholy. He only sought relief from the crack-up of his pouchy deteriorating body. In his last agony, there seems to have been nobody who could restrain him or help him, and nobody to admit responsibility for not being able to do so.

If Dylan had only lived latterly like the parody of a poet on the spree, he would have been forgotten. But these last years produced *Under Milk Wood*, a hymn to family and children and Laugharne, the sweetest of elegies for those he loved. Some criticised him later for deriving the ideas and images from the Circe episode in Joyce's *Ulysses*; but Dylan's play was no plagiarism. It was a metamorphosis of his Welsh experience. So was the dying fall of his last supreme poems of self-awareness, his 'Lament' for himself, his rage against dying on his father's behalf, and his own 'Poem On His Birthday', full of the joy of the mustardseed sun and the switchback sea, and the knowing that he would not reach forty years of age.

> . . . Oh, let me midlife mourn by the shrined
>   And druid herons' vows
> The voyage to ruin I must run,
>   Dawn ships clouted aground,
> Yet, though I cry with tumbledown tongue,
>   Count my blessings aloud . . .

> . . . And this last blessing most,
>   That the closer I move
> To death, one man through his sundered hulks,
>   The louder the sun blooms
> And the tusked, ramshackling sea exults . . .

Opposite: *Dylan, Caitlin and the dog Mably by Cliff Walk on the way to the Boat House, September 1953.*

Heritage and Legacy

Too many of the artists of Wales who go to live permanently in, for example, London, begin almost at once to anglicize themselves beyond recognition . . . On the other hand, too many of the artists of Wales stay in Wales too long, giants in the dark behind the parish pump, pygmies in the nationless sun, enviously sniping at the artists of other countries rather than attempting to raise the standard of art of their own country by working fervently at their own words, paint, or music.

And too many of the artists of Wales spend too much time talking about the position of the artists of Wales.

There is only one position for an artist anywhere: and that is, upright.

from 'Wales and the Artist', a broadcast by Dylan Thomas

Opposite: *Dylan directs a rehearsal of* Under Milk Wood *at the 'Y' in New York in May 1953.*

Heritage and Legacy

Dylan knew well the split in his education, reared by a schoolmaster who never spoke Welsh and who taught English in a sea-side halfway southern city that denied by tongue and habit the hard national heritage of the mountain valleys to the north. Yet Dylan called the problem of his divided inheritance unnecessarily, and trivially, difficult.

> There is a number of young Welshmen writing poems in English, who, insisting passionately that they are Welshmen, should by rights, be writing in Welsh, but who, unable to write in Welsh or reluctant to do so because of the un-commercial nature of the language, often give the impression that their writing in English is only a condescension to the influence and ubiquity of a tyrannous foreign tongue. I do not belong to that number . . . It's the poetry, written in the language which is most natural to the poet, that counts, not his continent, country, island, race, class, or political per-suasion.

The true question was, what was the language most natural to Dylan, what rhythm and structure of English? Dylan used to scoff at reviewers and critics who talked about the Welshness of his poetry, claiming in 1938 that he "never understood this racial talk, 'his Irish talent', 'undoubtedly Scotch inspiration', apart from whiskey." Yet, in fact, his ear for the rises and falls, stresses and syntaxes of local speech made him the heir of the bardic tradition in Wales, of the preacher and the poet of the people. He was also known to admit to the debt that all contemporary Anglo-Welsh writers had to the fierce Caradoc Evans, who had fought the first war of liberation against the philistinism and provincialism and chapel-strict standards of the pawky local literature before the time of Dylan, and who had attacked the Bible-black primness and hypocrisy of Welsh society and Nonconformity with the unadmitted biblical fervour of a true nonconformist. The young Dylan had visited him once at Aberystwyth with another Welsh writer, Glyn Jones. "We made a tour of the pubs in the evening, drinking to the eternal damnation of the Almighty and the soon-to-be-hoped-for destruction of the Tin Bethels. The university students love Caradoc, & pelt him with stones whenever he goes out."

Like the heretic, Dylan himself was indebted to the religion and history which he often seemed to attack. If he fled from the strictures of the chapels into the rich and sensuous world of the body, making the profane holy, he did it in the language of the King James's Bible, an influence he never denied. "Its great stories of Noah, Jonah, Lot, Moses, Jacob, David, Solomon, and a thousand more, I had, of course, known from very early youth; the great rhythms had rolled over me from the Welsh pulpits; and I read, for myself, from Job and Ecclesiastes; and the story of the New Testament is part of my life." If he had never sat down and studied the Bible or "consciously echoed its language", yet his childhood memories worked on that common property and quarry of all those who work in the English tongue.

In his piercing look at *The World of Dylan Thomas*, Clark Emery scrutinises the vocabulary of the collected poems, to discover that, after the paramount word 'I', the most frequent words are 'sea, man, love, like, sun, eye, as, time, lie, night, wind, water, light, sleep, over, green, moon, house, sky, turn, ghost, fire, grave, star, tree, white, world, stone, tongue, wound, see, sing, tell, still, summer, walk, word, seed, weather, voice, year, lover.' Most of these terms are Anglo-Saxon monosyllables; they usually deal with the actual and sensuous experience of a child. "Considered together, they have a pastoral quality somewhere between that of the Twenty-third Psalm and that of 'Anyone lived in a pretty how town'." The language was that of the sea-side child, surrounded by his family, intrigued by his body, protected by his home, rung awake by church bells. In the centre of it all, the selfish boy, sucking in all experience from Bible to back-chat, the "commoner than water" vocabulary of Swansea and Wales.

No more than he formally studied the Bible nor sorted out his experiences academically did Dylan consciously assimilate the traditions of the eisteddfods and the Welsh bards. These depended on a technical discipline controlling sound and rhythm, an internal repetition, and a successive use of parallel constructions. The *cynghanedd* or harmony of the formal poem was achieved by the sounds of multiple alliteration and internal rhymes. As Matthew Arnold noted in his criticism of

Welsh literature, the Celtic poet employed the utmost elaboration and often attained astounding skill in his work; but his content was rather short in interpretation of the world and long on sentiment, full of style and intensity, signifying not too much.

Dylan, however, took over, perhaps uncannily, the marvellous intricacy of the labours of the bards without losing a lyric frenzy and even a whole cosmogony. His last poems were his most elaborate, wrought in Laugharne according to the traditions of the unacknowledged land of his fathers. Gwyn Jones is correct when he says that Dylan was "Welsh in the cunning complexity of his metres, not only in the loose *cynghanedd*, the chime of consonants and pealing vowels, but in the relentless discipline of his verse, the hierarchic devotion to the poet's craft, the intellectual exactitude and emotional compression of word and phrase and stave and poem."

Read and listen to the care of it all, the lilt of letters, the sounds that soothe and words that awaken, the last lines of his last finished lyric poem, 'Prologue':

> We will ride out alone, and then,
> Under the stars of Wales,
> Cry, Multitudes of arks! Across
> The water lidded lands,
> Manned with their loves they'll move,
> Like wooden islands, hill to hill.
> Huloo, my proud dove with a flute!
> Ahoy, old, sea-legged fox,
> Tom tit and Dai mouse!
> My ark sings in the sun
> At God speeded summer's end
> And the flood flowers now.

Dylan, indeed, in his so-called 'Poetic Manifesto' of 1951, when he answered five questions put to him by a research student, testified to his obsession over his craft and profession, as careful as any bard. "I am a painstaking, conscientious, involved and devious craftsman in words, however unsuccessful the result so often appears, and to whatever wrong uses I may apply my technical paraphernalia, I use everything and anything to make my poems work and move in the directions I want them to: old tricks, new tricks, puns, portmanteau-words, paradox, allusion, paranomasia, paragram, catachresis, slang, assonantal rhymes, vowel rhymes, sprung rhythm. Every device there is in language is there to be used if you will. Poets have got to enjoy themselves sometimes, and the twistings and convolutions of words, the inventions and contrivances, are all part of the joy that is part of the painful, voluntary work."

Thus, willy-nilly, Dylan was a bard and a minstrel and a Welshman; even if he worked in an alien tongue, it was his natural tongue; he knew no other. As John Wain has pointed out, a Welsh poet, even an English monoglot, still does not feel, think or write like an English poet. "It is simply one of that huge category of truths which, though difficult or impossible to explain, are easy enough to see." Part of the explanation, however, is to be found in the importance given to the *spoken* word in Wales, the tradition of the *hwyl* and the *hiraeth*. The *hwyl* is the chanting sermon, the eloquent and intense and musical preaching that is the Welsh version of the gift of tongues. The *hiraeth* is the quality found in the mass singing of Welsh hymns, the spiritual force and longing of an ancient people, as expressed in a moving tribute to Dylan composed by the First Narrator in *Under Milk Wood* the first time it was put on in Laugharne after the poet's death:

I tarry in this cemetery of *hiraeth*
Not because he knew and loved his mother-tongue
Nor because he sang a selfless psalm in Salem.
He sought his bible in an English pub in English Laugharne
Playing a waiting game with words and gods . . .

Dylan himself always intoned and shouted, sang and mumbled his poems in English, before audiences and in the bath, boisterously and most privately in the toils of composition. The echo of the old preacher Marlais chanted in the voice of the poet bellowing against preachers, but in praise of his own special God. The bard worked on the hundreds of intricate drafts of the religious poems that looked to Blake and Donne rather than to ap Gwilym and W. H. Davies.

Dylan could not really understand the narrow and restricted output of either the 'court' bards who wrote in Welsh for the eisteddfods or the petty, although pretty, vision of such poets as W. H. Davies. When the young Dylan wrote his newspaper pieces on 'The Poets of Swansea' for the *Herald of Wales*, he called W. H. Davies the most gifted Welsh poet then writing in English, but he wondered why Davies had neglected the legends of his own country. "He could have recreated the fantastic world of the Mabinogion, surrounded the folk lore with his own fancies, and made his poetry a stepping place for the poor children of darkness to reach a saner world. . . ." Instead, Davies chose to be a hedgerow poet, describing the brevity of life, the green of the grass, and the inanity of personal expression. Although the older Dylan was to speak more kindly of Davies, praising the inevitability in his slightest verses and the unique observations in his tiniest reflections on the natural world, he never really approved of a poet who chose to be a miniaturist and refused to strike out for the wilder shores of creation.

By his work and refusal to restrict himself to being a Welsh poet with a local reputation, Dylan advanced and popularised the writings of a whole group of his Anglo-Welsh contemporaries, particularly his friend Vernon Watkins, and Gwyn Jones, Glyn Jones, R. S. Thomas, Gwyn Thomas, and Alun Lewis. If Caradoc Evans fought a local war of liberation, Dylan Thomas led an international guerrilla attack on the classicism of Eliot and Auden and on the intellectual and critical dominance of London, Oxford, Cambridge, and Harvard. His romantic revolt unleashed a certain coarseness and richness of language, a revelling in comedy and bawdry, an affirmation of the holy myths rather than a snivelling at God, an orgy of the irrational as opposed to the careful classification of what was meaningful or significant.

Gwyn Jones has described the contemporaries and followers of Dylan. "Bible-blest and chapel-haunted, wrestle hard as we can, we stand confessed the last, lost nonconformists of an Age." Dylan helped them to make their way as men of letters, since his revolt was the most extreme and original of them all. Yet he, too, never escaped that first puritan training, that sense of sin, that holy infusion of childhood. He was more at home with Vaughan and Blake than with Marx and Proust. As that brilliant commentator on Dylan, John Ackerman, has stressed continually, Dylan's bardic qualities, prophetic and intuitive, eloquent and religious, rhetorical and intricate, made him grow in Gwyn Jones's words "from dragon's tooth to druid in his own land".

Yet some elements in modern Wales and some critics disliked him for his Englishness and his sensuousness. Bourgeois and chapel society found him shocking and irreverent, while the stricter Welsh Nationalists found him an Uncle Tom in *Under Milk Wood*, feeding the B.B.C. with the fond pap and sentimental follies so dear to foreign gawpers in search of Welsh antics. This attack was joined by such moralistic and uncomprehending critics as David Holbrook, who considers Dylan's attitude to the people of Llaregyb that "of the week-ender from

Opposite: *Laugharne.*

sophisticated London, his country people toys in a model farmyard." Such profound misunderstanding of Dylan's aims and purposes often hid its righteousness under an assault on his unreality, when his purpose was to conjure up the irrational forces of nostalgia and dream and pastoral, the human joy in the sensual base of love, and the human grief at the death which must lie behind it.

Other critics condemned Dylan for writing with a perverse brilliance in a stepmother tongue. One did not see his imagery as a renewal of the English language, but as "the *revenge* taken by a conquered race on the self-satisfied culture of its conquerors." Dylan's efforts to introduce some bardic discipline and internal rhyming and alliteration, especially in poems such as 'The Conversation Of Prayer', were a dead end rather than a new influence. Dylan had, indeed, condemned over-indulgence in strict bardic forms, stating that it succeeded only "in warping, crabbing and obscuring the natural genius of the English language." Yet the interplay between form and rhythm, strictness and looseness, the use of every trick of language in the poet's box, was the very strength and tension of Dylan's poetry; there never was a total surrender to sound as in the worst of Swinburne, never to a straitjacket of metre as in the worst of Auden or Graves.

Dylan loved Wales and sang its countryside more clearly than any other bard or minstrel had done. He also loved its towns and the little city of Swansea, and wrote comic and sad plays and stories about them that seemed to catch their essence in the opinions of most people who lived there or visited there. Yet Dylan's very ease of final style after his labours, his success with a mass audience as well as on the Third Programme, seemed to attract envy like flies round melting ice-cream on Swansea beach. He never had any time for academic critics when he was alive, not only from fear of seeming ignorant to them, but also from boredom at their niggling. As Caitlin knew, he hated pretension as well as "every type of flowery excursion into intellectualism . . . he had the same dislike, amounting to superstitious horror, of philosophy, psychology, analysis, criticism; all those vaguely termed ponderous tomes; but most of all, of the gentle art of discussing poetry. . . "

An unkind critic himself, Dylan only liked the intellectual company of working poets of the better sort, who managed to write criticism now and again. He grew out of his early lack of generosity towards his peers. That had been very much a defence of his Swansea youth, mere provincial bravado, as was the unreal destruction of his family's home by his alter ego, Samuel Bennet, in *Adventures in the Skin Trade*. In a

St David's Head, Pembrokeshire, 1953: one of the last photographs of Dylan and Caitlin.

recent perceptive essay, Walford Davies has restated what Dylan always knew, Cwmdonkin Drive was a refuge and an escape for him from the world, as Laugharne was to be later. "The street was a safe hole in a wall behind the wind in another country." The young dog and the old dog remained convention-bound and convention-ridden, however much they railed against convention. As Caitlin also wrote, "though Dylan imagined himself to be completely emancipated from his family background, there was a very strong puritanical streak in him, that his friends never suspected; but of which I got the disapproving benefit." On one occasion in Soho, he literally tore the flesh off his hands with his nails, crying, "To get at the bone, and then to get rid of that! What a wonderful thing!" Calvin and Wesley would have understood that action.

Suburban and sick of it until he needed a retreat from the city, puritan and rebellious in the stewpots until he needed to write and recuperate, Dylan merely reversed the face of Swansea as he saw it. He was not prim outside and lecherous within, chapel to his world and brothel to his dream. He flaunted his revolt and hid his strict decencies. "One: I am a Welshman", he boasted in Rome in 1947; "two: I am a drunkard; three: I am a lover of the human race, especially of women." In fact, one: he was a poet; but the other priorities followed in that order, Welshness first.

This appreciation of Dylan Thomas has tried to show that he was born to a divided bardic tradition, a bi-lingual speech, a split-minded people, a provincial bias; only his home was safe, first with his parents, finally with Caitlin, the womb with a view. Once secure in the Welsh suburb or country, he longed for the city; once disgusted by the city or foreign parts, he yearned for the deathful peace of Wales. Two letters, one to Bert Trick in 1939 from Laugharne, one to Margaret Taylor in 1947 from Rapallo, prove this thesis and antithesis in his restless goings. In Laugharne, he wrote, "I miss the boys and the smoky nights. Here everything is so slow and prettily sad. I'd like to live in a town or a city again for a bit. Let there be one town left, and we'll fill it with ourselves." Yet, from Italy, he was to write back, "Oh, anywhere a house. I am lost without one. I am domestic as a slipper, I want somewhere of my own, I'm old enough now, I want a house to shout, sleep, and work in." So he bounced from home to away, from security to exposure, until the blood ran thin in him as the alcohol rose.

Vernon Watkins, who probably knew Dylan best of all other than Caitlin, has written that any study of him must remain totally inadequate. For he prized seriousness and was a born clown. He created an immediate intimacy with strangers and hid his private strict self. "The entertainer and the intellectual alike were slightly ashamed after meeting him, as he could beat them both at their own game; but if they were humble, they quickly recognised that he was humble too. The prig was his *bête noir*, the pedant a black and white crosswood figure whom he didn't despise. The variety of life and its abundance sang in his veins. He was born to praise it and he did so most completely when war distorted it into every manifestation of horror." After the war, as Watkins further said, Dylan's own war continued. His free and easy social life led to the rich comedy of the broadcasts; his isolation and fear and toil to the intricacy of the later poems. Yet the social mask put on to protect the inward poet was fatal. "His method was not to retreat from the mask but to advance beyond it, and in that exaggeration remain completely himself. He agreed readily with his detractors and did not at all mind being misunderstood. Then, in the private dark, his exuberance was subjected to the strictest control."

So the contradictions of the man who was the finest lyric poet of his age; one foot in Eden, the other in Babylon; one hand in the Bible, the other under the bedclothes; his heavy head lifted to the sky, his feet on the bar-rail; a frail angel become gross, a self-declared Lucifer who took in his aged parents; the sensuous prophet of the adolescent, the generous wastrel of middle age, the fierce mourner of the dead; a first name from the *Mabinogion* that he passed on to a folk-singer, a last name so common in Wales that it meant any farmer, railwayman, teacher or housewife; the bard of the mysteries of heaven and hell, the poet of the country and the body, the writer of the excessive and the vernacular. His plays shall sound for him, his poems shall speak for him as long as there are ears to hear. Let him be his own last best witness.

> Man himself is a work. Today he is a dirty piece of work.
> But tomorrow he may sprout wings under his serge shoulders,
> be faced and sided like Aquarius, who is the first sign of the
> vital year.

So much for Dylan's hope for humanity, and finally, for his hope for himself.

> . . . And every wave of the way
> And gale I tackle, the whole world then,
> With more triumphant faith
> That ever was since the world was said,
> Spins its morning of praise,
>
> I hear the bouncing hills
> Grow larked and greener at berry brown
> Fall and the dew larks sing
> Taller this thunderclap spring, and how
> More spanned with angels ride
> The mansouled fiery islands! Oh,
> Holier then their eyes,
> And my shining men no more alone
> As I sail out to die.

Fishguard Bay

Dylan on Dylan

Dylan on Dylan

Three times in his life, Dylan Thomas answered a set of questions about his attitude to poetry. The first was at the age of nineteen, the second at the age of thirty-one, the last at the age of thirty-six, three years before the poet's early death. In the replies to these questions, a comparison can be made between the poet's changing feelings towards his craft and to his awareness of himself.

The first of his answers was written to New Verse *and printed in October, 1934. It reflects much of his ambivalence at the time. While he strongly asserts that his poetry reflects his individual struggle from darkness towards some measure of light and thus declares his distance from the socially-committed poetry of Auden and his school, yet he does put himself on the side of a form of Marxist control of the means of production, in order to make possible communal art. He supports the narrative poem from tradition, justifying it by reference to T. S. Eliot and rejecting any form of Surrealist poem by association. He also rejects spontaneous creation, pointing out the hard labour of his craft. His claim to the influence of Freud is probably lip-service. Dylan's images at the time seem largely the product of his subconscious without benefit of self-analysis on the Freudian model.*

The Answers to *New Verse* (1934)

1. Do you intend your poetry to be useful to yourself or others?

To both. Poetry is the rhythmic, inevitably narrative, movement from
an overclothed blindness to a naked vision that depends, in its intensity,
on the strength of the labour put into the creation of the poetry. My
poetry is, or should be, useful to me for one reason: it is the record of
my individual struggle from darkness towards some measure of light,
and what of the individual struggle is still to come benefits by the
sight and knowledge of the faults and fewer merits in that concrete
record. My poetry is, or should be, useful to others for its individual
recording of that same struggle with which they are necessarily
acquainted.

2. Do you think there can now be a use for narrative poetry?

Yes. Narrative is essential. Much of the flat, abstract poetry of the present
has no narrative movement, no movement at all, and is consequently
dead. There must be a progressive line, or theme, of movement in every
poem. The more subjective a poem, the clearer the narrative line.
Narrative, in its widest sense, satisfies what Eliot, talking of 'meaning',
calls 'one habit of the reader'. Let the narrative take that one logical
habit of the reader along with its movement, and the essence of the poem
will do its work on him.

3. Do you wait for a spontaneous impulse before writing a poem;
if so, is this impulse verbal or visual?

No. The writing of a poem is, to me, the physical and mental task of
constructing a formally watertight compartment of words, preferably
with a main moving column (i.e., narrative) to hold a little of the real
causes and forces of the creative brain and body. The causes and forces
are always there, and always need a concrete expression. To me, the
poetical 'impulse' or 'inspiration' is only the sudden, and generally
physical, coming of energy to the constructional, craftsman ability.
The laziest workman receives the fewest impulses. And vice versa.

4. Have you been influenced by Freud and how do you regard him?

Yes. Whatever is hidden should be made naked. To be stripped of darkness is to be clean, to strip off darkness is to make clean. Poetry, recording the stripping of the individual darkness, must inevitably cast light upon what has been hidden for too long, and, by so doing, make clean the naked exposure. Freud cast light on a little of the darkness he had exposed. Benefiting by the sight of the light and the knowledge of the hidden nakedness, poetry must drag further into the clean nakedness of light more even of the hidden causes than Freud could realise.

5. Do you take your stand with any political or politico-economic party or creed?

I take my stand with any revolutionary body that asserts it to be the right of all men to share, equally and impartially, every production of man from man and from the sources of production at man's disposal, for only through such an essentially revolutionary body can there be the possibility of a communal art.

6. As a poet what distinguishes you, do you think, from an ordinary man?

Only the use of the medium of poetry to express the causes and forces which are the same in all men.

Opposite: *Portrait of Dylan Thomas by Augustus John.*

Dylan's next set of answers was more poignant, as he was being hounded by creditors and was deeply in debt by the end of the Second World War. Horizon magazine, edited by Cyril Connolly, had sent him a set of questions on 'The Cost of Letters', which it printed in its issue of September, 1946. The replies reflected both Dylan's sensibility towards the times – less Marxist now, more a matter of the Welfare State – and his wish to slough off his financial problems onto a patron, the government or a private Maecenas. He more strongly stresses the urge of the poet for individual freedom, and he defends the necessity of earning money for a family by taking on a second job. His regret is that he can no longer live cheaply enough to survive by his own art. Yet he advises young and hopeful writers to write. His personal disillusion has never extended to his chosen profession.

The Answers to 'The Cost of Letters' (1946)

1. How much do you think a writer needs to live on?

He needs as much money as he wants to spend. It is after his housing, his feeding, his warming, his clothing, the nursing of his children, etc., have been seen to – and these should be seen to by the State – that he really needs money to spend on all the luxurious necessities. Or, it is then that he doesn't need money because he can do without those necessary luxuries. How much money depends, quite obviously, on how much he wants to buy. I *want* a lot, but whether I *need* what I want is another question.

2. Do you think a serious writer can earn this sum by his writing,
and if so, how?

A serious writer (I suppose by this you mean a good writer, who might be comic) can earn enough money by writing seriously, or comically, if his appetites, social and sensual, are very small. If those appetites are big or biggish, he cannot earn, by writing what he wishes to write, enough to satisfy them. So he has to earn money in another way: by writing what he doesn't want to write, or by having quite another job.

3. If not, what do you think is the suitable second occupation for him?

It's no good, I suppose, saying that I know a couple of good writers who are happy writing, for a living, what they don't particularly want to write, and also a few good writers who are happy (always qualified by words I'm not going to use now) being bank clerks, Civil Servants, etc. I can't say how a writer can make money most suitably. It depends on how much money he wants and on how much he wants it and on what he is willing to do to get it. I myself get about a quarter of the money I want by writing what I don't want to write and at the same time trying to, and often succeeding in, enjoying it. Shadily living by one's literary wits is as good a way of making too little money as any other, so long as, all the time you are writing B.B.C. and film scripts, reviews, etc., you aren't thinking, sincerely, that this work is depriving the world of a great poem or a great story. Great, or at any rate very good, poems and stories do get written in spite of the fact that the writers of them spend much of their waking time doing entirely different things. And even a poet like Yeats, who was made by patronage financially safe so that he need not write and think nothing but poetry, *had*, voluntarily, to give himself a secondary job: that of philosopher, mystic, crank, quack.

4. Do you think literature suffers from the diversion of a writer's energy into other employments or is it enriched by it?

No, to both questions. It neither suffers nor is it enriched. Poems, for instance, are pieces of hard craftsmanship made interesting to craftsmen in the same job, by the work put into them, and made interesting to everybody, which includes those craftsmen, by divine accidents: however taut, inevitably in order, a good poem may appear, it must be so constructed that it is wide open, at any second, to receive the accidental miracle which makes a work of craftsmanship a work of art.

5. Do you think the State or any other institution should do more for writers?

The State should do no more for writers than it should do for any other person who lives in it. The State should give shelter, food, warmth, etc., whether the person works for the State or not. Choice of work, and the money that comes from it, should then be free for that man; what work, what money, is his own bother.

6. Are you satisfied with your own solution of the problem and have you any specific advice to give to young people who wish to earn their living by writing?

Yes and No, or *vice versa*. My advice to young people who wish to earn their living by writing is: DO.

Opposite: *Dylan Thomas in 1947.*

A research student asked Dylan Thomas the answers to five questions on one of the American lecture tours. The replies were recorded and eventually published in the Texas Quarterly, Winter, 1961, *under the heading of 'Poetic Manifesto'. The interview is the most revealing one given by the mature poet, and it is less self-conscious than his talks for the B.B.C. on his poetry.*

In the interview, Dylan testifies to the influence of sound *on his poetry, to the noises and voices of childhood, to the sensuous nuances of words before they had meanings for him, to the rhythms of spoken Welsh and biblical language. Out of this jumble of reasoned nonsense came the expressed depths and passions and humour of living. Among the list of his influences, those of his childhood listed in his answer to the first question are certainly true, but in the second answer, he downgrades the influence of Joyce on himself for fear of being thought something of a plagiarist of* Portrait of the Artist as a Young Man *in his own sketches of autobiographical youth, and of many sequences of* Ulysses *which seem to serve as the inspiration of passages in* Under Milk Wood. *Dylan is honest now about the second-hand influence of Freud on his work – an unconscious, although real, influence on his own Unconscious. He again emphasises his work at poetry, and he now delivers a swingeing and open attack on the Surrealists – too fashionable in 1934 for such a frontal assault. He concludes with an exhortation which showed his true unselfishness, his urge to communicate the* love *of poetry to everybody who would hear him, and his final understanding of the need to celebrate God.*

The Answers called 'Poetic Manifesto' (1951)

You want to know why and how I first began to write poetry, and which poets or kind of poetry I was first moved and influenced by.

To answer the first part of this question, I should say I wanted to write poetry in the beginning because I had fallen in love with words. The first poems I knew were nursery rhymes, and before I could read them for myself I had come to love just the words of them, the words alone. What the words stood for, symbolised, or meant, was of very secondary importance; what mattered was the *sound* of them as I heard them for the first time on the lips of the remote and incomprehensible grown-ups who seemed, for some reason, to be living in my world. And these words were, to me, as the notes of bells, the sounds of musical instruments, the noises of wind, sea, and rain, the rattle of milkcarts, the clopping of hooves on cobbles, the fingering of branches on a window pane, might be to someone, deaf from birth, who has miraculously found his hearing. I did not care what the words said, overmuch, nor what happened to Jack & Jill & the Mother Goose rest of them; I cared for the shapes of sound that their names, and the words describing their actions, made in my ears; I cared for the colours the words cast on my eyes. I realise that I may be, as I think back all that way, romanticising my reactions to the simple and beautiful words of those pure poems; but that is all I can honestly remember, however much time might have falsified my memory. I fell in love – that is the only expression I can think of – at once, and am still at the mercy of words, though sometimes now, knowing a little of their behaviour very well, I think I can influence them slightly and have even learned to beat them now and then, which they appear to enjoy. I tumbled for words at once. And, when I began to read the nursery rhymes for myself, and, later, to read other verses and ballads, I knew that I had discovered the most important things, to me, that could be ever. There they were, seemingly lifeless, made only of black and white, but out of them, out of their own being, came love and terror and pity and pain and wonder and all the other vague abstractions that make our ephemeral lives dangerous, great, and bearable. Out of them came the gusts and grunts and hiccups and heehaws of the common fun of the earth; and though what the words meant was, in its own way, often deliciously funny enough, so much funnier seemed to me, at that almost forgotten time, the shape and shade and

Dylan Thomas in about 1950.

size and noise of the words as they hummed, strummed, jigged and galloped along. That was the time of innocence; words burst upon me, unencumbered by trivial or portentous association; words were their spring-like selves, fresh with Eden's dew, as they flew out of the air. They made their own original associations as they sprang and shone. The words, 'Ride a cock-horse to Banbury Cross', were as haunting to me, who did not know then what a cock-horse was nor cared a damn where Banbury Cross might be, as, much later, were such lines as

John Donne's, 'Go and catch a falling star, Get with child a mandrake
root', which also I could not understand when I first read them. And
as I read more and more, and it was not all verse, by any means, my
love for the real life of words increased until I knew that I must live
with them and *in* them, always. I knew, in fact, that I must be a writer
of words, and nothing else. The first thing was to feel and know their
sound and substance; what I was going to do with those words, what
use I was going to make of them, what I was going to *say* through them,
would come later. I knew I had to know them most intimately in all
their forms and moods, their ups and downs, their chops and changes,
their needs and demands. (Here, I am afraid, I am beginning to talk too
vaguely. I do not like writing *about* words, because then I often use
bad and wrong and stale and woolly words. What I like to do is to treat
words as a craftsman does his wood or stone or what-have-you, to hew,
carve, mould, coil, polish and plane them into patterns, sequences,
sculptures, fugues of sound expressing some lyrical impulse, some
spiritual doubt or conviction, some dimly-realised truth I must try to
reach and realise.) It was when I was very young, and just at school,
that, in my father's study, before homework that was never done, I
began to know one kind of writing from another, one kind of goodness,
one kind of badness. My first, and greatest, liberty was that of being
able to read everything and anything I cared to. I read indiscriminately,
and with my eyes hanging out. I could never have dreamt that there
were such goings-on in the world between the covers of books, such
sand-storms and ice-blasts of words, such slashing of humbug, and
humbug too, such staggering peace, such enormous laughter, such and
so many blinding bright lights breaking across the just-awaking wits
and splashing all over the pages in a million bits and pieces all of which
were words, words, words, and each of which was alive forever in its
own delight and glory and oddity and light. (I must try not to make
these supposedly helpful notes as confusing as my poems themselves.)
I wrote endless imitations, though I never thought them to be imitations
but, rather, wonderfully original things, like eggs laid by tigers. They
were imitations of anything I happened to be reading at the time:
Sir Thomas Browne, de Quincey, Henry Newbolt, the Ballads, Blake,
Baroness Orczy, Marlowe, Chums, the Imagists, the Bible, Poe, Keats,
Lawrence, Anon., and Shakespeare. A mixed lot, as you see, and
randomly remembered. I tried my callow hand at almost every poetical
form. How could I learn the tricks of a trade unless I tried to do them
myself? I learned that the bad tricks come easily; and the good ones,

229

which help you to say what you think you wish to say in the most meaningful, moving way, I am still learning. (But in earnest company you must call these tricks by other names, such as technical devices, prosodic experiments, etc.)

The writers, then, who influenced my earliest poems and stories were, quite simply and truthfully, all the writers I was reading at the time, and, as you see from a specimen list higher up the page, they ranged from writers of school-boy adventure yarns to incomparable and inimitable masters like Blake. That is, when I began, bad writing had as much influence on my stuff as good. The bad influences I tried to remove and renounce bit by bit, shadow by shadow, echo by echo, through trial and error, through delight and disgust and misgiving, as I came to love words more and to hate the heavy hands that knocked them about, the thick tongues that had no feel for their multitudinous tastes, the dull and botching hacks who flattened them out into a colourless and insipid paste, the pedants who made them moribund and pompous as themselves. Let me say that the things that first made me love language and want to work *in* it and *for* it were nursery rhymes and folk tales, the Scottish Ballads, a few lines of hymns, the most famous Bible stories and the rhythms of the Bible, Blake's *Songs of Innocence*, and the quite incomprehensible magical majesty and nonsense of Shakespeare heard, read, and near-murdered in the first forms of my school.

You ask me, next, if it is true that three of the dominant influences on my published prose and poetry are Joyce, the Bible, and Freud. (I purposely say my 'published' prose and poetry, as in the preceding pages I have been talking about the primary influences upon my very first and forever unpublishable juvenilia.) I cannot say that I have been 'influenced' by Joyce, whom I enormously admire and whose *Ulysses*, and earlier stories I have read a great deal. I think this Joyce question arose because somebody once, in print, remarked on the closeness of the title of my book of short stories, *Portrait of the Artist As a Young Dog* to Joyce's title, *Portrait of the Artist as a Young Man*. As you know, the name given to innumerable portrait paintings by their artists is, 'Portrait of the Artist as a Young Man' – a perfectly straightforward title. Joyce used the painting title for the first time as the title of a literary work. I myself made a bit of doggish fun of the *painting*-title and, of course, intended no possible reference to Joyce. I do not think that Joyce has had any hand at all in my writing; certainly his *Ulysses* has not. On the other hand, I cannot deny that the shaping of some of my *Portrait* stories might owe something to Joyce's stories in the volume, *Dubliners*. But then *Dubliners* was a pioneering work in the world of the short story, and no good storywriter since can have failed, in some way, however little, to have benefited by it.

The Bible, I have referred to in attempting to answer your first question. Its great stories of Noah, Jonah, Lot, Moses, Jacob, David, Solomon and a thousand more, I had, of course, known from very early youth; the great rhythms had rolled over me from the Welsh pulpits; and I read, for myself, from Job and Ecclesiastes; and the story of the New Testament is part of my life. But I have never sat down and studied the Bible, never consciously echoed its language, and am, in reality, as ignorant of it as most brought-up Christians. All of the Bible that I use in my work is remembered from childhood, and is the common property of all who were brought up in English-speaking communities. Nowhere, indeed, in all my writing, do I use any knowledge which is not commonplace to any literate person. I *have* used a few difficult words in early poems, but they are easily looked-up and were, in any case, thrown into the poems in a kind of adolescent showing-off which I hope I have now discarded.

And that leads me to the third 'dominant influence': Sigmund Freud. My only acquaintance with the theories and discoveries of Dr Freud has been through the work of novelists who have been excited by his case-book histories, of popular newspaper scientific-potboilers who have, I imagine, vulgarised his work beyond recognition, and of a few modern poets, including Auden, who have attempted to use psycho-analytical phraseology and theory in some of their poems. I have read only one book of Freud's, *The Interpretation of Dreams*, and do not recall having been influenced by it in any way. Again, no honest writer today can possibly avoid being influenced by Freud through his pioneering work into the Unconscious and by the influence of those discoveries on the scientific, philosophic, and artistic work of his contemporaries: but not, by any means, necessarily through Freud's own writing.

To your third question – Do I deliberately utilise devices of rhyme, rhythm, and word-formation in my writing – I must, of course, answer with an immediate, Yes. I am a painstaking, conscientious, involved and devious craftsman in words, however unsuccessful the result so often appears, and to whatever wrong uses I may apply my technical

paraphernalia, I use everything and anything to make my poems work
and move in the directions I want them to: old tricks, new tricks, puns,
portmanteau-words, paradox, allusion, paranomasia, paragram,
catachresis, slang, assonantal rhymes, vowel rhymes, sprung rhythm.
Every device there is in language is there to be used if you will. Poets
have got to enjoy themselves sometimes, and the twistings and convolutions of words, the inventions and contrivances, are all part of the
joy that is part of the painful, voluntary work.

Your next question asks whether my use of combinations of words to
create something new, 'in the Surrealist way', is according to a set
formula or is spontaneous.

There is a confusion here, for the Surrealists' set formula was to
juxtapose the unpremeditated.

Let me make it clearer if I can. The Surrealists – (that is, super-
realists, or those who work *above* realism) – were a coterie of painters
and writers in Paris, in the nineteen twenties, who did not believe in
the conscious selection of images. To put it in another way: They were
artists who were dissatisfied with both the realists – (roughly speaking,
those who tried to put down in paint and words an actual representation
of what they imagined to be the real world in which they lived) – and
the impressionists who, roughly speaking again, were those who tried
to give an impression of what they imagined to be the real world. The
Surrealists wanted to dive into the subconscious mind, the mind
below the conscious surface, and dig up their images from there
without the aid of logic or reason, and put them down, illogically and
unreasonably, in paint and words. The Surrealists affirmed that, as
three-quarters of the mind was submerged, it was the function of the
artist to gather his material from the greatest, submerged mass of the
mind rather than from that quarter of the mind which, like the tip of
an iceberg, protruded from the subconscious sea. One method the
Surrealists used in their poetry was to juxtapose words and images
that had no rational relationship; and out of this they hoped to achieve a
kind of subconscious, or dream, poetry that would be truer to the real,
imaginative world of the mind, mostly submerged, than is the poetry
of the conscious mind that relies upon the rational and logical relationship of ideas, objects, and images.

This is, very crudely, the credo of the Surrealists, and one with which
I profoundly disagree. I do not mind from where the images of a poem
are dragged up: drag them up, if you like, from the nethermost sea of

the hidden self; but before they reach paper, they must go through all the rational processes of the intellect. The Surrealists, on the other hand, put their words down together on paper exactly as they emerge from chaos; they do not shape these words or put them in order; to them, chaos is the shape and order. This seems to me to be exceedingly presumptuous; the Surrealists imagine that whatever they dredge from their subconscious selves and put down in paint or in words must, essentially, be of some interest or value. I deny this. One of the arts of the poet is to make comprehensible and articulate what might emerge from subconscious sources; one of the great main uses of the intellect is to *select*, from the amorphous mass of subconscious images, those that will best further his imaginative purpose, which is to write the best poem he can.

And question five is, God help us, what is my definition of Poetry?

I, myself, do not read poetry for anything but pleasure. I read only the poems I like. This means, of course, that I have to read a lot of poems I don't like before I find the ones I do, but, when I *do* find the ones I do, then all I can say is, 'Here they are', and read them to myself for pleasure.

Read the poems you like reading. Don't bother whether they're 'important', or if they'll live. What does it matter what poetry *is*, after all? If you want a definition of poetry, say: 'Poetry is what makes me laugh or cry or yawn, what makes my toenails twinkle, what makes me want to do this or that or nothing', and let it go at that. All that matters about poetry is the enjoyment of it, however tragic it may be. All that matters is the eternal movement behind it, the vast undercurrent of human grief, folly, pretension, exaltation, or ignorance, however unlofty the intention of the poem.

You can tear a poem apart to see what makes it technically tick, and say to yourself, when the works are laid out before you, the vowels, the consonants, the rhymes or rhythms, 'Yes, this is *it*. This is why the poem moves me so. It is because of the craftsmanship.' But you're back again where you began.

You're back with the mystery of having been moved by words. The best craftsmanship always leaves holes and gaps in the works of the poem so that something that is *not* in the poem can creep, crawl, flash, or thunder in.

The joy and function of poetry is, and was, the celebration of man, which is also the celebration of God.

Acknowledgments

The publishers wish to express their thanks to the following museums, libraries, archives, agencies and individuals from whose collections photographs have been reproduced. With special thanks to Christina Gascoigne for her photography of Wales commissioned for this book.

Bunny Adler courtesy of Rollie McKenna, 167; Michael Ayrton, 138 (collection John Arlott); The Bettmann Archive, 221; Bill Brandt, 128; John Deakin/The Condé Nast Publications Limited, 187; Christina Gascoigne, back jacket, 15, 20–21, 23, 29, 40–41, 65, 72–73, 80, 100–101, 103, 124–125, 162–163, 170–171, 183, 188, 190, 211, 216–217; The Glynn Vivian Art Gallery and Museum Swansea, 62; Geoffrey Grigson, 89; Gwynedd County Archives Caernarvon, 10; G. D. Hackett, New York, 229; Pamela Hansford Johnson, 37, 60; Richard Hughes, 97, 152; Tal L. Jones courtesy Time Inc., 174; The Poetry Collection of the Lockwood Memorial Library State University of New York at Buffalo, endpapers; Rollie McKenna, half-title, title, 6, 9, 16, 26, 54, 105, 130, 154–155, 157, 165, 168, 173, 177, 178–179, 181, 184, 185, 194, 196, 197, 198, 200, 202, 204, 234–235; Lee Miller Penrose/The Condé Nast Publications Limited, 116, 159, 225; by permission of The National Museum of Wales Cardiff, front jacket, 45, 57, 84, 92; The National Portrait Gallery London, 71, 112; origin unknown, 19, 47, 48, 59, 127, 148; Popperfoto, 119, 132, 133; photo. Douglas Glass, 151; The Radio Times Hulton Picture Library, 76, 94, 109, 110, 123, 135, 142, 145, 147; Bill Read, 213; Nora Summers courtesy of Rollie McKenna, 32, 39, 98, 107; The Swansea Daily Post and Herald of Wales, 149; Timon Films Limited, 69; Mrs Mary Treece, 87.

Every possible care has been taken to acknowledge the correct sources for the photographs reproduced in this book; however the publishers wish to apologise to anyone whose copyright they may have unknowingly infringed.

The publishers acknowledge with gratitude New Directions Publishing Corporation, Dylan Thomas's usual American publishers, for permission to reprint extracts from his work published in America, and to the following writers and publishers for permission to reprint extracts from the material listed below:

B. T. Batsford Limited, *Welsh Country Upbringing*, 1948 by D. Parry Jones. J. M. Dent and Sons Limited, *Dylan Thomas: The Poems*, edited by Daniel Jones, 1971; *Quite Early One Morning*, 1954 broadcasts by Dylan Thomas; *Portrait of the Artist as a Young Dog*, 1940 Dylan Thomas; *A Prospect of the Sea*, 1955 Dylan Thomas; *The Map of Love*, 1939 Dylan Thomas; *The Doctor and the Devils*, 1953 Dylan Thomas; *The Life of Dylan Thomas*, 1965 by Constantine Fitzgibbon; *Selected Letters by Dylan Thomas* edited by Constantine Fitzgibbon, 1966. Faber and Faber Limited, Dylan Thomas *Letters to Vernon Watkins*, 1957. Pamela Hansford Johnson from *Adam International Review No. 236*, 1953. Gwyn Jones, "*Welsh Dylan*" from *Adelphi*, February 1954. Mervyn Levy, "*A Womb with a View*" from *John O'London*, November 1962. The Poetry Collection of the Lockwood Memorial Library at the State University of New York at Buffalo, "*How Shall My Animal*" from the *1930 Notebook*; "*From Love's First Fever to Her Plague*" from the *August 1930 Notebook*; "*Within His Head Revolved A Little World*" from the *February 1933 Notebook*. The London Magazine, September 1957 "*Recollections of Dylan Thomas*" by Geoffrey Grigson. Random House Incorporated, *In Defence of Ignorance*, 1955 by Karl Shapiro. The Texas Quarterly IV Winter 1961, *Poetic Manifesto*. Caitlin Thomas, *Leftover Life to Kill*, 1957; *Not Quite Posthumous Letter to My Daughter*, 1963, Putnam and Company Limited. Triton Publishing Company Limited and McGraw-Hill Book Company, *Me and My Bike*, 1965 Dylan Thomas. Rosalind Wade passages from the *Parton Street Poets*.

The publishers also wish to express their special thanks to David Higham Associates, the agents for Dylan Thomas and his literary executors, for kindly giving permission to quote extensively from the work of Dylan Thomas, and for permission to quote from the work of Vernon Watkins and Gwyn Thomas.

1	2	3	4	5	6	7	8	9	10
11	12	13	14	15	16	17	18	19	20
21	22	23	24	25	26	27	28	29	30
31	32	33	34	35	36	37	38	39	40
41	42	43	44	45	46	47	48	49	50
51	52	53	54	55	56	57	58	59	60
61	62	63	64	65	66	67	68	69	70
71	72	73	74	75	76	77	78	79	80
81	82	83	84	85	86	87	88	89	90
91	92	93	94	95	96	97	98	99	100
101	102	103	104	105	106	107	108	109	110
111	112	113	114	115	116	117	118	119	120
121	122	123	124	125	126	127	128	129	130
131	132	133	134	135	136	137	138	139	140
141	142	143	144	145	146	147	148	149	150
151	152	153	154	155	156	157	158	159	160
161	162	163	164	165	166	167	168	169	170
171	172	173	174	175	176	177	178	179	180
181	182	183	184	185	186	187	188	189	190
191	192	193	194	195	196	197	198	199	200
201	202	203	204	205	206	207	208	209	210
211	212	213	214	215	216	217	218	219	220
221	222	223	224	225	226	227	228	229	230
231	232	233	234	235	236	237	238	239	240
241	242	243	244	245	246	247	248	249	250
251	252	253	254	255	256	257	258	259	260
261	262	263	264	265	266	267	268	269	270
271	272	273	274	275	276	277	278	279	280
281	282	283	284	285	286	287	288	289	290
291	292	293	294	295	296	297	298	299	300
301	302	303	304	305	306	307	308	309	310
311	312	313	314	315	316	317	318	319	320
321	322	323	324	325	326	327	328	329	330
331	332	333	334	335	336	337	338	339	340
341	342	343	344	345	346	347	348	349	350
351	352	353	354	355	356	357	358	359	360
361	362	363	364	365	366	367	368	369	370
371	372	373	374	375	376	377	378	379	380
381	382	383	384	385	386	387	388	389	390
391	392	393	394	395	396	397	398	399	400